CULTURES OF THE WORLD

TUNISIA

Roslind Varghese Brown

MARSHALL CAVENDISH
New York • London • Sydney

Reference edition published 1998 by
Marshall Cavendish Corporation
99 White Plains Road
Tarrytown
New York 10591

© Times Editions Pte Ltd 1998

Originated and designed by
Times Books International, an imprint of
Times Editions Pte Ltd

Printed in Singapore

Library of Congress Cataloging-in-Publication Data:
Brown, Roslind Varghese.
    Tunisia / Roslind Varghese Brown.
      p. cm.—(Cultures of the World)
    Includes bibliographical references and index.
    Summary: Examines the history, economy, people,
lifestyles, and culture of this Arab country in northern Africa.
    ISBN 0-7614-0690-5 (library binding)
    1. Tunisia—Juvenile literature. [1. Tunisia.] I. Title.
II. Series.
DT245b.B76   1998
961.1—dc21   97–15883
               CIP
               AC

INTRODUCTION

THE REPUBLIC OF TUNISIA is a country of diversity and pleasant contradictions. Part of the Maghrib, a group of Arab countries in North Africa, Tunisia is strongly influenced by its location on the Mediterranean coast and by its French colonial heritage. Tunisia's population is 98 percent Muslim, but the country has a secular government. Tourism is an important economic sector and most tourists are European and American travelers.

Cultures of the World Tunisia looks at the diverse lifestyles of the country, from the highly educated elite to the seminomadic tribes who still live as they did in ancient times. The book examines Tunisia's history from the time Phoenicians founded a trading post in Carthage in the 9th century B.C. up to the close of the 20th century. In particular, this book traces Tunisia's progress since independence, revealing how this relatively young country has developed a thriving economy, while keeping in check extremist elements that threaten to upset the country's gains in the modern world.

CONTENTS

Children of the desert—
a Berber child carrying a
lamb.

CONTENTS

Puppets on sale in Tunis.

GEOGRAPHY

TUNISIA, SITUATED ON THE NORTHERNMOST TIP of North Africa, is a wedge of land between Algeria and Libya. Lying almost in the center of the southern Mediterranean sea coast, Tunisia is 90 miles (145 km) southwest of Sicily. Through conquest and territorial proximity, Tunisia has been influenced by African, European, and Arab cultures, and Tunisians are a blend of these peoples. The Arabs called the region of North Africa under their control the *Maghrib*, or the Arab West. At one time the Maghrib included Morocco, Algeria, Tunisia, Tripolitania (northwest Libya), and Mauritania.

Tunisia has a land area of 63,378 square miles (164,419 square km), approximately the size of the state of Missouri. Nearly half of its total boundary is coastline. Tunis, the capital, lies on the northern coast.

Tunisia can be divided into three parts: the mountainous north, the central steppes, and the desert south.

Its location on the Mediterranean Sea, midway between the Straits of Gibraltar and the Suez Canal, made Tunisia an important stopping point for traders in the early seafaring days. The gulfs of Tunis, Hammamet, and Gabès provided excellent natural harbors for warships and trading vessels. These features made Tunisia very attractive to early conquerors.

Left: **Boats moored at the port of Mahdia between the gulfs of Hammamet and Gabès.**

Opposite: **A caravan journey across the Sahara. Tunisia lies between the Mediterranean coast to the north and the desert to the south.**

TOPOGRAPHY

MOUNTAINOUS NORTH Occupying a quarter of the total land area, the mountainous north consists of two chains that are extensions of the Atlas Mountains of Algeria: the Northern Tell, or Tell, made up of the Kroumirie and Mogod mountains and the High Tell or Dorsale (a word meaning "backbone"). The Northern Tell is more rugged than the Dorsale, but since both are made chiefly of soft sandstone and limestone, they have a lower, rounded profile compared with the sharp outlines of the Atlas Mountains west of Tunisia.

The few peaks reaching 5,000 feet (1,500 m) are found in the Dorsale, near the Algerian border. The highest recorded peak is Djebel Chambi (5,066 feet/1,543 m). The Medjerda, Teboursouk, and Tebessa mountains in the Dorsale divide Tunisia into two distinct climatic regions: the well-watered, Mediterranean north and the semiarid, desert south.

Tunisia's longest and only river with a year-round flow of water is the Medjerda, which flows between the Northern Tell and the Dorsale. Rising

TUNISIA—THE BEGINNING OF "AFRICA"

"Ifriqiyah" is a name that is believed to be the root of "Africa." Historians offer other possible sources of the name:

faraqa—from the Carthaginian word meaning colony, used to describe the areas outside the city of Carthage

Afer (plural, *Ifri*)—from the name of a Berber tribe

Afar—Arabic for "the land"

Ifrikos—Philistine name for the son of Goliath, the giant named in the Bible

When the Arab conquerors came in the 7th century A.D. they called Tunisia *Ifriqyya*, while the rest of the African continent was called *Africa–Ifriqyya*. Only from the Middle Ages did the names "Tunis" and "Tunisia" begin to appear on world maps.

in the Medjerda mountains of northeast Algeria, it flows 286 miles (460 km) eastward to the Gulf of Tunis. The Medjerda River is used extensively for irrigation and to produce hydroelectric power, and its tributaries form the principal river system in Tunisia. The Medjerda valley is richly covered with alluvium, making it extremely fertile. It has been the richest grain-producing region of the country since the period of Roman rule.

Blessed with the richest soil of the country and a gentle climate, the mountainous north produces most of Tunisia's agricultural crops and is home to 50 percent of its population.

CENTRAL STEPPES South of the mountains are plateaus ranging from 600 to 1,500 feet (180–450 m); elevations decrease toward the east. This semiarid region is named according to elevation: from west to east, high steppes, low steppes, and the Sahel along the eastern coast. The high steppes are broad alluvial basins between low

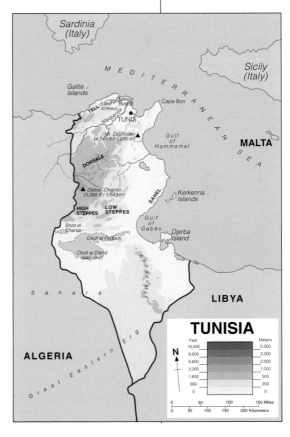

Chott el Djérid, the largest salt lake in Tunisia, covers 1,900 square miles (4,900 square km). In the winter a chott fills with water that later evaporates, leaving a thick salt crust on the surface for most of the year.

mountains, and the low steppes are flat, gravel-covered plateaus. The Sahel includes a 200-mile (320-km) coastal strip and the islands of Djerba and Kerkenna. It has two distinct climatic areas: the northern, well-watered coast along the Gulf of Hammamet and the southern, drier region along the Gulf of Gabès.

SOUTHERN DESERT Tunisia's desert begins just south of the steppes and merges into the Sahara. The desert is bordered by an extensive depression containing three seasonal *chotts* or salt lakes: Chott el Djérid, Chott el Gharsa, and Chott el Fedjadj. In the high ground around the chotts, date palms grow abundantly in oases.

Tunisia's desert spreads over nearly half its total land area, yet it forms only a tiny fraction of the Sahara, a bleak, desolate wasteland covering a quarter of Africa. The desert terrain is characterized by drifting sand dunes from Algeria's Grand Erg Oriental, rocky areas, and mountain ridges of the flat-topped Ksour Mountains in the east. With the exception of scattered oases supplied by underground water, the southern desert is barren land.

CLIMATE

Tunisia's climate is determined by the Mediterranean Sea, which brings cool breezes and moisture to the north, and the Sahara, which sends hot, dusty winds blowing across the south. The climate varies in accordance with the three distinct terrains of mountains, steppes, and desert.

The mountainous north has mild, wet winters (October to April) and hot, dry summers (May to September). Pleasant most of the time, the winters can be uncomfortable since central heating was introduced only recently and is available only in newer buildings. Temperatures average 45°F (7°C) in January and 80°F (27°C) in July. Rainfall averages 16–39 inches (40–100 cm) annually and occurs mainly in the winter.

The semiarid central steppes have little, unpredictable rainfall. Here, summers are hot and winters mild. Rainfall averages 8–16 inches (20–40 cm) annually and occurs mainly in winter. Temperatures on the coast or Sahel are moderated by the sea breezes, but the northern coast is cooler and wetter than the south, which is influenced by desert heat a few miles inland.

The temperature range is much greater in the desert, where summers are hotter and winters colder than elsewhere in Tunisia. Burning hot days (often over 100°F/38°C) are followed by cool evenings and cold nights. Rainfall is low, at 4–8 inches (10–20 cm) annually. Hot southerly winds called sirocco (or *chehili* in Tunisia) bring dreaded, blinding blizzards of sand blowing in from the Sahara.

The fields and orchards of the Enfida plain of the northern Sahel, near the Gulf of Hammamet.

FLORA AND FAUNA

THE NORTH The cool, wet north, blessed with rich soil irrigated all year round by the Medjerda River, is the agricultural hub of the country. Crops grown here include wheat, olives, grapes, citrus fruit, jasmine (for perfume), pistachios, jujube, and gum. The mountains are covered with wild juniper, myrtle, and laurel. The Kroumirie mountains of northwest Tunisia are famous for their forests of cork oak.

The forested Northern Tell is the hunting ground of wild boars and jackals. In the Dorsale, the sleeved mouflon and gazelles are seen. Migratory birds flying south from Europe in the fall include aquatic and wading birds such as ducks, egrets, flamingos, geese, herons, and storks. Rapid urban expansion in northern Tunisia may result in a reduced number of migratory birds, particularly those that favor secluded habitats.

THE CENTRAL AND COASTAL REGIONS In the arid steppes, where the soil is poor, wild esparto grass is grown for the manufacture of paper and rope. Cereal grains, date palms, and olive trees are also cultivated in oases. There is little vegetation for animals other than nomadic herds of sheep, goats, and camels. Nomads use two kinds of camel: a stockier species to carry loads and a long-legged one that moves fast.

The warm waters of Tunisia's coast, especially in the Gulf of Gabès, have more than 80 species of fish—including gilthead, sole, tuna, bonito, and shark—and sponges, octopuses, and shellfish. The northern coast is a coral haven for shrimps and lobsters. Monk seals are a protected species in the northern island sanctuary of Galite off the coastal town of Tabarka.

THE DESERT At oases, date palms grow in abundance, but elsewhere in the desert there is very little plant life. Plants that have adapted to the

Tunisian desert include the acacia with its long roots, scrub grass, saltbush, and cacti that store water in their fleshy stems. Ants, scarabs (a beetle species), scorpions, horned vipers, cobras, and lizards like the skink and dab are common in the Sahara. Small animals include the fennec and the jerboa, called the kangaroo rat because of its strong hind legs. Buzzards can be found in the desert and migratory birds stop at oases.

EXTINCTION OF WILDLIFE

In the early 20th century, lions and panthers were still being hunted in the northern mountains, but the destruction of habitats through soil erosion, deforestation, overgrazing, and excessive fuel gathering has endangered several species of wildlife. The Barbary hyena, Barbary leopard, and Mediterranean monkey seal were declared endangered in 1987. By 1994, six mammal species, 14 bird species, and 26 plant species were classified as endangered. Through the help of the World Wildlife Fund, the Atlas deer was rescued from near extinction. Today the leopard, cheetah, scimitar-horned oryx, and the Moroccan dorcas gazelle are nonexistent in Tunisia.

MAJOR CITIES AND HISTORICAL SITES

Many of Tunisia's cities were founded centuries ago. The older section of a Tunisian city, called the medina, is a walled area filled with a labyrinth of passageways lined with shops, houses, and mosques. Tunisia's major cities, besides the capital Tunis, are Sfax, Sousse, Bizerte, and Kairouan.

TUNIS The economic and cultural capital of Tunisia, Tunis is also the most important port. It is built on Tunis Lake, which is connected to the Mediterranean by a man-made channel. Tunis was a small settlement during the Phoenician period and the early years of Arab rule. It was made a capital city under the Hafsids, a 13th century Arab dynasty. In 1535 Spain,

Tunis has 700,000 people, but the area called Greater Tunis—including La Goulette, Carthage, La Marsa, Gammarth, Ben Arous, and Hamman Lif— is populated by an estimated two million.

then at war with the Ottoman empire, took possession of Tunis. The Turks repossessed it from 1539 until 1881, except for two years from 1573 to 1574, when Tunis was again occupied by Spain. Tunis became the capital of independent Tunisia in 1956.

A gateway called Bab el-Bahar leads into the medina of Tunis. It was called "Sea Gate" when the Mediterranean Sea was believed to have come right up to it. New Tunis lies beyond this gate, built mostly on land reclaimed from the sea by the French during their rule from 1881 to 1956. Tunis is continually developing, and the pattern of settlement is uneven. One-third of the population prefer to be crammed into the old and small medina, while the remaining two-thirds are evenly distributed between makeshift homes on the outskirts of Tunis, built for nomads and those in search of jobs in the city, and the new city built by the French. The rich live comfortably in Belvedere, a former royal park situated a few miles from the city, well provided by superb garden landscaping, waterfront cafés, a zoo, the Museum of Modern Art, a swimming pool, and a stadium.

Leading from the Bab el-Bahar is the famous Avenue Habib Bourguiba, the hub of modern Tunis and the site of its major buildings. Named after Tunisia's independence leader and president for 31 years, Avenue Habib Bourguiba was renamed Avenue 7 Novembre years after he was ousted on November 7, 1987.

THE BARDO MUSEUM

Bardo Palace was the residence of the *beys* (rulers) until 1957. The palace building complex now includes the Bardo Museum, the National Assembly, and an old arsenal. The famous Bardo Museum exhibits artifacts from various periods of Tunisian history that have been excavated from historical sites in Tunisia. Many of the collections are named after the location of the excavations; for example there are Mahdia, Sousse, and Carthage rooms. Bardo Museum is known especially for its Carthaginian collection and its rich Roman and Byzantine mosaics. The only known portrait of the Latin poet Virgil is found here, in a mosaic measuring 1,475 square feet (137 square meters). This is believed to be the largest mosaic portrait in existence.

In the collection devoted to Tunisia's early history is the Hermaion monument from the Middle Paleolithic era (c. 40,000 B.C.). This monument, a pyramid of stone balls, carved flints, and animal bones, is dedicated to the spirit of a stream.

The Roman and pre-Christian exhibits include ornamental tiling from the first church in Tunisia dating to the 4th century A.D.; statues of the ancient Greek and Roman gods Apollo, Asclepius, and Ceres; a 3rd century A.D. mosaic of the Greek god Dionysus giving a vine to a peasant; and Roman funerary glassware, pottery, and statuettes.

The Islamic collection contains beautiful books of calligraphy including the blue Kairouan Koran, which is embellished with gold writing.

SFAX This coastal city opposite the Kerkenna Islands is the second largest city in Tunisia and a metropolis of the south. It is an economic center with a prominent commercial port, and it is important as an industrial, agricultural, and fishing town.

Talented architects have built futuristic buildings in the new sections of town to rival the work of their competitors in Tunis. Jokes that tell of this competition exist in abundance, although with the migration of southerners to the northern capital city, this competitiveness is less intense. Sfax became prosperous during Roman rule through growing, pressing, and shipping olive oil to its Mediterranean neighbors. This wealthy city caters to tourists with first class hotels, shops, cafés, restaurants, and grand buildings. The 11th century Great Mosque has one of the finest minarets in Tunisia.

SOUSSE Tunisia's third largest city, 80 miles (130 km) north of Sfax and on the Gulf of Hammamet, began as Hadrumetum, a Phoenician town founded in the 9th century B.C. The name Sousse is derived from "Susah," the Berber name for the town. Sousse, a thriving port and very popular seaside resort known for its white beaches, is often referred to as the "pearl of the coast." An abundance of leisure activities are offered including diving, horseback-riding, sailing, and golfing. Like many other Tunisian cities, Sousse has an intriguing blend of old and new sections. The museum, which is second in importance only to the Bardo Museum in Tunis, has collections that trace scenes from the Roman and Byzantine periods (from the first to the sixth centuries A.D).

The waterfront town of Sousse with its *ribat*, or fortress (right). Muslim rulers built such fortresses to defend their coastal cities from Christian warriors. Sousse was particularly vulnerable to attack as it had no natural land defenses.

Above: **Destroyed twice in the 8th century, Kairouan's Great Mosque was rebuilt and developed by succeeding Muslim rulers in the 9th century. Much of the 9th century work remains today.**

Opposite: **Courtyard of the Barber's mosque in Kairouan, site of the tomb of Prophet Mohammed's companion. He was known as the barber because he always carried with him three hairs of the Prophet's beard.**

BIZERTE Its strategic location at the northernmost point in North Africa after the Straits of Gibraltar decided Bizerte's destiny as a military outpost. Bizerte was known as Hippo Diarrhytus in Phoenician and Roman times, and its modern name was given by the Arabs when they conquered it in the seventh century A.D. When Tunisia became a French protectorate a channel was built linking Lake Bizerte to the Mediterranean, making Bizerte a naval base. Bizerte's military role ended in 1963 when the French naval base was evacuated and the city returned to independent Tunisia.

KAIROUAN About 80 miles (130 km) south of Tunis lies Kairouan, the fourth most important Islamic city in the world, after Mecca, Medina, and Jerusalem. Seven visits to Kairouan are equivalent to one pilgrimage to Mecca.

Kairouan was founded in A.D. 670 by Uqba ibn Nafi, whose armies entered North Africa from the south on a quest to conquer territory and spread Islam to the Maghrib. Kairouan, surrounded by salt lakes and dry land, was an inhospitable place. Muslims believe that when the city was founded, a miraculous stream appeared at the bottom of a well, filling it with water from the Zem Zem spring in Mecca, thousands of miles away.

Kairouan is famous for its beautiful, imposing mosques and the centuries-old art of carpet weaving. The city's main attraction is the Great Mosque, the first mosque built in North Africa by the conqueror Uqba ibn Nafi in the 7th century A.D. to house Arabic, Greek, and Islamic literature. Seven doors in the fortress-like walls open into the courtyard to reveal the mosque's amazing beauty. From the white marbled courtyard, one enters a prayer room through one of 17 carved cedar doors leading to a forest of 414 multicolored marble and porphyry columns.

"Qairwan," the Arabic name for Kairouan, may be the source of the term "caravan." This Islamic city was strategically located on the caravan trail linking Egypt with the Maghrib.

BULLA REGIA This is an ancient town built in tiers on the slopes of a mountain some 25 miles (40 km) southwest of Béja, a town along the Medjerda River. Many ruins remain here, including Roman baths, the temples of Apollo and Isis, a theater, a Byzantian Christian basilica and baptistry, and unusual underground houses with names such as Palaces of Hunting and Fishing and the House of the Peacock.

CAPE BON PENINSULA This peninsula in the northeast has exotic gardens, thermal springs with curative powers, beaches, and popular shopping areas. Hammamet and Nabeul are two towns on the peninsula.

Nabeul is famous for its arts and crafts, particularly cane and esparto mats, ceramics with enameled yellow and green designs, orange flower water, and embroidered cloth. The Museum of Nabeul has rare statues and earthenware dating to the 7th century B.C. and a fine collection of antique lamps, ceramics, and mosaics. Nabeul is at its prettiest in spring when the trees are in full bloom. The city celebrates spring with a festival of orange blossoms around the end of March and early April.

Hammamet, a small seaside resort town lined with citrus trees, is south of Nabeul. Its sandy white beaches and warm weather attract Europeans and Tunisians on vacation. The medina is especially pleasing, being painted in pastel colors. Homes have wooden doors the same color as the walls, but each door has a unique design of decorative studs. Behind the doors are gardens with fountains and ceramic-decorated archways.

The wealthy own villas in Hammamet with a view of the gulf.

CARTHAGE—A WOMAN'S FIND

A legend surrounds the founding of the ancient Phoenician city of Carthage by Elissa-Dido, the shrewd queen of Tyre (in modern Lebanon). She fled from her brother, King Pygmalion, in the 9th century B.C., after he murdered her husband. Arriving in the region of Carthage, she tricked the inhabitants into giving her land: they agreed she could have land that did not exceed the size of a cow's hide. She outwitted them by cutting the hide into thousands of fine strips, which she tied end-to-end to form an extremely long rope to encircle the Hill of Byrsa. Carthage or Kart-Hadasht (Phoenician for "New City") was founded in 814 B.C.

Carthage became the first naval power in the Mediterranean to conquer parts of Spain and Italy and expand into Africa. This strategic control of the Mediterranean threatened Roman supremacy and resulted in three wars with Rome (the Punic Wars). After the final battle, the victorious Romans razed the city and covered the site with salt so no crops could grow. The survivors were deported.

Roman baths in Carthage, believed to be the largest in the world. A century after the Romans destroyed Carthage, Julius Caesar ordered the rebuilding of the city, and so well was this accomplished that Carthage became the third most important city of the Roman empire after Rome and Alexandria.

HISTORY

ARCHEOLOGISTS HAVE EXCAVATED stone tools two million years old in the Maghrib. In the early Stone Age, inhabitants of Tunisia were hunters, fishers, growers, and gatherers. Little else is known of their existence before the Phoenicians arrived in the 12th century B.C. Historical events in Tunisia since then have been influenced by its strategic position along the Mediterranean sea route between Europe and Asia.

Phoenician traders established settlements on Tunisia's northeast coast. One of them, Carthage, a settlement founded in the 9th century B.C., grew to encompass most of present-day Tunisia by the 6th century B.C. This challenged Rome, another contender for Mediterranean supremacy, and Carthage changed hands in the 2nd century B.C. It stayed under Roman rule until the 5th century A.D., when the Vandals and later the Byzantines came to power.

In the 7th century A.D. the Arabs brought Islam to Tunisia; it was the beginning of five Arab dynasties there. Regardless of who controlled the area since, Tunisia has remained an important part of the Islamic world. In the beginning of the 16th century, the Spanish commanded some coastal areas, speeding up the decline of the last Arab dynasty. The Ottoman Turks conquered the territory and held it until their own decline in the late 19th century.

A political tustle in Europe for strategic control over Tunisia ended with France making Tunisia a French protectorate in 1881. Tunisia became a self-governing country on July 25, 1957.

Above: **Phoenician gravestones in a museum in Carthage.**

Opposite: **Roman ruins at Dougga, in northern Tunisia.**

Hannibal's overland trek was a remarkable feat. A 26,000-man army on foot or mounted on horses or elephants crossed the Pyrenees and the Alps. This illustration shows his army crossing the Rhone River.

PHOENICIAN RULE

In the 12th century B.C. Phoenicians from Tyre established settlements on the North African coast to service their ships sailing between Tyre and Spain, a source of tin and silver. According to legend, in 814 B.C. Dido founded a settlement in North Africa called Kart-Hadasht, or Carthage. Unlike the other Phoenician settlements, Carthage was politically independent. It grew powerful partly in response to Greek attempts to drive the Phoenicians from Sicily. By the 3rd century B.C., Carthage controlled Sicily, Sardinia, Corsica, Spain, and Africa. Fearful of this rival power in the Mediterranean, Rome began a campaign against Carthage. The Punic Wars that resulted spanned 118 years.

FIRST PUNIC WAR (264–241 B.C.) Rome's opportunity came in 264 B.C. when Messina and Syracuse, two Sicilian cities, quarreled over Messina. Carthage settled the dispute and occupied Messina, but a Roman army forced the Carthaginians to withdraw. Rome took over Corsica in 260 B.C., and four years later established its army at Clypea in Africa (modern Kélibia). Plagued by internal revolts, Carthage nonetheless repelled the Romans in 256 B.C. At last, in 241 B.C., with a superior fleet of 200 warships, Rome was victorious.

In the next two decades Rome captured Carthaginian territory in Corsica and Sardinia without retaliation, but Carthage began to extend its empire into Spain, where General Hamilcar Barca founded Alicante and Barcino (modern Barcelona). Two Carthaginian leaders succeeded Hamilcar—his son Hannibal and son-in-law Hasdrubal. In 219 B.C., Hannibal captured Saguntum in Spain, and Rome once again declared war.

SECOND PUNIC WAR (218–201 B.C.) The Romans controlled the sea, so Hannibal crossed overland to Italy in 218 B.C. His army inflicted costly losses on the Roman empire, capturing Capua. The Romans blocked reinforcements led by Hasdrubal and recaptured Capua in 211 B.C. In 203 B.C., Hannibal returned to Africa. Meanwhile, the Romans turned on Carthaginian strongholds in Spain and northern Africa. Carthage was defeated in Spain by 206 B.C., and Hannibal's army was defeated at Zama in Africa in 202 B.C. Carthage was forced to pay huge reparations to Rome.

THIRD PUNIC WAR (149–146 B.C.) The Carthaginians recovered their prosperity and paid off their debt in 10 years. A vengeful Rome found an excuse for war when Carthage broke the peace agreement in 150 B.C. by going to war with Rome's ally, the Numidian prince Massinissa. After three years, a besieged Carthage fell in eight days of fierce fighting.

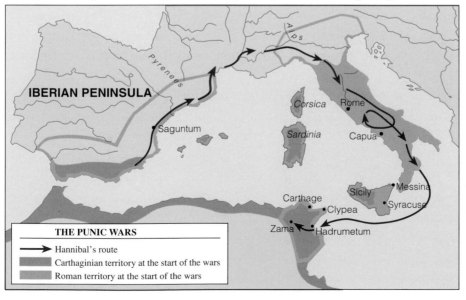

The Punic Wars lasted 118 years, with Mediterranean territory changing hands at various points. At the very end of the third Punic War, Carthage reportedly burned for 17 days.

IBERIAN PENINSULA

Pyrenees

Alps

Corsica
Rome
Sardinia
Capua
Saguntum

Carthage
Sicily
Messina
Clypea
Syracuse
Zama
Hadrumetum

THE PUNIC WARS
→ Hannibal's route
Carthaginian territory at the start of the wars
Roman territory at the start of the wars

ROMAN RULE

A Roman proconsul ruled Rome's proconsular province, which included modern Tunisia and part of Libya and Algeria. To defend the province, guarded boundaries known as "limes" stretched from Libya to Morocco, across southern Tunisia. Within these boundaries, the Roman army kept the peace and promoted agriculture, which had replaced trade in importance. Roman engineers designed aqueducts to bring water from the mountains to the coast to irrigate the land for crops of wheat, grapes, and olives. Tunisia became the granary of Rome. Estates mushroomed with landlords leasing out land to tenants who paid rent and taxes.

In Rome, Christianity became the official religion with the publication of the Thessalonian edict in A.D. 380, when Theodosius (379–395) was emperor. During the reign of his successors, the Roman empire began to decline. By that time it had split into the eastern and western empires, ruled from Byzantium (later Constantinople) and Rome. Poor leadership and lack of support in the proconsular province caused the decline of Roman control in northern Africa in the 6th century A.D.

VANDALS

Plagued by internal troubles, the Romans could not defend the province from the Vandals, who entered North Africa in A.D. 429 under King Gaiseric (428–477). These Germanic warriors—Aryan Christians who wore horsehair jackets and lived in tents—initially coexisted with the Romans. In 339 Gaiseric conquered Carthage and established Vandal rule in North Africa.

From his capital in Carthage, Gaiseric ruled North Africa, Sardinia, Sicily, Corsica, and the Balearic Islands. In A.D. 455 the Vandals invaded and looted Rome. In A.D. 476, in a second Vandal attack on Rome, the last Roman emperor Romulus Augustulus was executed, ending the western Roman empire and (for a while) Roman control of North Africa. Persecution of Roman Catholic Christians by the Vandals increased under Huneric (477–484), who succeeded Gaiseric.

THE BYZANTINES

After the breakup of the western Roman empire, the eastern Roman empire survived as the Byzantine empire. The Byzantine emperor Justinian reconquered North Africa in the 6th century, bringing it back under Roman rule. When Gelimer took the throne from Hilderich, Huneric's son and Justinian's ally, Justinian sent his armies to Tunisia and Gelimer was defeated in A.D. 534. The Byzantines made little attempt to improve people's living conditions. They also tried to promote the Byzantine style of Christianity, which featured elaborate ceremonies. These factors incited Berber opposition, opening a door to a powerful external force—Islam.

Although the term "vandalism" comes from "Vandals," they were not the first or the last conquerors to loot and destroy property.

27

ARAB MUSLIM RULE

Islam, a religion that teaches the word of God as revealed to the Prophet Mohammed, began in the early seventh century A.D. There were three waves of Islamic expansion before the Arabs conquered Roman Africa—Ifriqyya in Arabic. It was during the fifth caliph's reign that the Arabs invaded Ifriqyya under the leadership of emir (commander) Uqba ibn Nafi. Various Arabic dynasties controlled Tunisia as part of their extended empire.

UMAYYAD RULE (661–750) Uqba ibn Nafi made Kairouan a base from which to conquer Byzantine territory in Ifriqyya. It was a good location, being separated from the Byzantine cities on the coast and the Berber strongholds of resistance in the Numibian mountains. At first, the Arabs coexisted with the Berbers, converting some of them, but their aim was to rule northern Africa. Uqba died in 682 in a battle against an army of Berbers and Byzantines. An Arab army sent out of Egypt in 693 eventually subdued a Berber army led by a woman, Kahinah, in 698. Carthage—the Byzantine center—fell to the Arabs soon after. Arab successes on land and on the Mediterranean Sea overcame remnants of Byzantine resistance by the turn of the century.

From his capital in Damascus, Syria, the Umayyad caliph ruled over the Maghrib. The Umayyads introduced an Islamic system where religious judges ruled over all matters of law, guided by the Koran, the holy book of Islam, and sayings of the Prophet. The Arabs were interested in spreading their culture, but freedom of religion was allowed and military

The Abbasids added square minarets to the Great Mosque in Kairouan. They also favored the use of bricks.

28

service was overlooked for a tax that went toward the welfare of the poor. Within the security that the Arabs created, trade flourished. Not surprisingly, the people welcomed them as liberators and protectors. Through intermarriage, Arab culture and Islam spread rapidly. But trouble was brewing. Many Berbers converted to Islam and joined military service to avoid taxes, but the Arabs did not accept the converts as equals. Berber soldiers, for example, received less pay than Arab soldiers.

A movement arose in Morocco to oppose Arab leadership. The Kharijite Berbers there questioned the selection of caliphs based on race, station, or descent from the Prophet. The Berbers in Ifriqyya joined the Kharijites and invaded Kairouan. Islamic tribal kingdoms were established. During this period of turmoil the Umayyad dynasty in Damascus declined. In 750 Abu al Abbas (a descendant of Abbas, the Prophet's uncle) became the next caliph. He began the Abbasid dynasty and moved the capital to Baghdad, Iraq.

Much of the fighting in the Abbasid period took place during the rule of Caliph Haroun al Rashid (786–809), who was made famous by the book, *The Arabian Nights*.

ABBASID RULE (750–800) The Abbasid period was a turbulent one, and the Abbasids often lost control of North Africa to the rebellious Kharijite Berbers. On two occasions they even had to fight to regain their military base at Kairouan. It was not until the end of the eighth century that order was restored to Ifriqyya. In A.D. 800 the Abbasid caliph passed local government to emirs (commanders), who still had to report to the caliph in Baghdad. Ibrahim ibn al-Aghlab was appointed emir to Ifriqyya and he started the hereditary Aghlabid dynasty.

The *ribat* (fortress) at Monastir was built by the Aghlabids, who made it a religious center and a site visited by Muslim pilgrims. The Aghlabids built fine mosques and walled towns. The Aghlabid period is believed to be Ifriqyya's golden age.

AGHLABID RULE (800–909) Although they were under the caliphate in Baghdad, the Aghlabids ruled Ifriqyya as an independent state. Under the third Aghlabid ruler, Ziyadat Allah I (817–838), attacks on Byzantine-held Sicily began in A.D. 827, and over the next 75 years the Aghlabids conquered all of Sicily. For a while the Aghlabids had control of Sardinia and southern Italy as well, giving the Arabs supremacy over the Byzantines.

By the early 10th century the Aghlabids' power had declined, and the Fatimids took control. Since the 7th century, two Islamic groups developed that remain until today: the Sunni and Shi'a. The Shi'a believe only direct descendants of the Prophet should rule. The Sunni believe Islamic rulers should be elected from among the Prophet's descendants. The Abbasids were Sunnis, as were the Aghlabids. The religious leaders they elected were often proud nobles who did not identify with the poor non-Arabs. This created resentment, and when taxes became a burden, opposition grew among the Berbers, who supported the Fatimids, a Shi'a group that claimed descent from Fatima, the Prophet's daughter.

FATIMID RULE (910–1044) 'Ubayd Allah al-Mahdi, who founded the Fatimid dynasty, fled from Syria to escape Sunni oppression. He reached Tunisia in A.D. 909 and by 910 had declared himself caliph in his capital of Kairouan, renouncing the caliphate in Baghdad.

Fatimid rule was harsh and intolerant, but trade developed quickly. European demand for Eastern goods made Fatimid-controlled areas in Ifriqyya and Sicily important distribution centers. Trading houses opened all over Ifriqyya, dealing in spices, lacquer, dyes, grain, drugs, and cloth woven from Egyptian flax.

'Ubayd's successors enlisted the help of an influential Zirid Berber chief to quell opposition from the extremist Kharijite and Sunni Berbers. The Fatimids gave the Zirid leader, Yusuf Bulukkin ibn Ziri, control over the Maghrib while they themselves concentrated on Egypt and new territory. Thus began the first Berber dynasty under the Zirids—the first group native to Tunisia to control Ifriqyya where the majority of the people were Berbers.

Interior of the 'Ubayd Allah Mosque in Mahdia. In 921 'Ubayd moved his capital to Mahdia. The Fatimids spread their control over the Maghrib and into Egypt, founding Cairo in 969. Cairo became the new capital of the Shi'a caliphate that rivaled the Shi'a caliphate in Baghdad.

SCHOLARSHIP IN KAIROUAN

Kairouan became the center of religious, cultural, and intellectual influence. It was a market for Hebrew and Arabic books on many subjects that were copied by scribes. Greek translations of Arabic texts on science and philosophy were introduced to Europe over the next 200 years. The scholar Ibn Abi Zayd al-Qayrawani (d. 996) codified the Malikite school of Islamic law that applied throughout the Maghrib, and he wrote more that 40 volumes on the science or philosophy of law.

The Almoravids and Almohads, two rival tribal dynasties in Morocco, collectively ruled over the Maghrib and Muslim Spain for 200 years. During Almohad rule Moorish culture began to develop, and unique forms of art, architecture, and literature were created.

BERBER CONTROL

ZIRID RULE (1044–1148) The Zirids neglected the economy. Agricultural production declined and farmers and herdsmen resorted to crime. To gain the support of rich Arabs, Zirid rulers switched from Shi'aism to Sunnism in 1044. The betrayal brought swift retribution—the Fatimids sent Bedouin tribes out of Egypt, and as they moved through Ifriqyya, the Bedouin destroyed towns and turned fertile ground into grazing land for their herds.

In the midst of these tribulations, Christian control returned to Ifriqyya through Europeans from southern Italy who invaded Sicily, then occupied Djerba Island in 1134. They eventually controlled the coastal towns. Another Berber dynasty, the Almohads, moved in from Morocco, conquering territories in the Maghrib and forcing out the Europeans in 1160.

ALMOHAD RULE (1160–1207) Under the Almohad ruler Abd al Mumin, the Maghrib was once more unified under Berber control. Ibn Tumart, a Sunni Muslim who started the Almohad dynasty, was a religious reformer. After a short period, their control over their empire declined, and the Almohads appointed a viceroy, Mohamed ben Abu Hafs, who established the Hafsid dynasty. When the Almohad dynasty fell in Morocco, Hafsid rulers adopted the titles of caliph and sultan.

HAFSID RULE (1207–1574) Abu Zakariya al Hafs moved the capital from Kairouan to Tunis, and Ifriqyya was renamed Tunisia. The Hafsids concentrated on the coastal towns, coexisting with the Berbers by leaving the inland areas to them. Stability returned to Tunisia. Trade links were developed and ambassadors exchanged with European states. There was a cultural revival, and the Zituna Mosque in Tunis, with its library of 36,000 Islamic texts, became the center of Islamic learning in the Maghrib.

Les turs.

Hafsid ties with Europe worsened in 1270 during the crusade led by French King Louis IX. Internal conflicts later weakened the Hafsids. In the 15th century, the war between Spain and the Ottoman Turks was brought to Tunis. The Hafsids supported the Spanish in a battle that lasted 50 years.

BARBAROSSA THE PIRATE Frederick Barbarossa—Khair al din to the Muslims and Redbeard to the Europeans—and his brother Aruj were Greek Muslims. In 1504 they reached Tunisia with Hafsid support. In 1510 the ruler of Algiers asked the brothers to defend it from the Spanish. Instead, they conquered Algiers and made it their base for piracy.

The Barbarossas recognized the supreme authority of the Ottoman sultan. Frederick was appointed the sultan's regent in the Maghrib with the title *beylerbey* (commander-in-chief). This made the pirates enemies of the Hafsids, who were resisting Ottoman control. After three attempts, Tunis was captured in 1574 and the last Hasfid ruler was brought to Constantinople. Tunisia became a Turkish province ruled by the beylerbey in Algiers.

A 16th century woodcut of King Louis' disembarkation at Carthage. The Europeans captured Carthage, but a plague killed the king and many of his men.

A 16th century miniature of Janissaries, an elite Turkish military unit.

RULE OF THE OTTOMAN TURKS

The Ottomans divided the Maghrib into administrative units called regencies. The regency of Tunis was headed by a governor called a *pasha*, who was allowed no political power. The Janissaries kept order and reported to officers called *dey*. The dey collected taxes in the coastal towns, while a civilian bey controlled Berber tribes inland with a private army. The bey of Tunis was the effective ruler of Tunisia, although Tunisia remained part of the Ottoman empire until the French takeover.

HUSSEINID DYNASTY (1709–1957) In the 17th and 18th centuries there was conflict with the tribal areas and with Algiers, another regency which made many attempts to control Tunisia. Hussein ibn Ali, who won the loyalty and support of the Berbers and the religious and military leaders, defeated the Algerian forces and started the Husseinid dynasty in 1709. Hussein, a Greek, was a Mamluk, a non-Turkish subject in lifetime service with the Ottoman empire. Powerful government positions were reserved for Mamluk officers and the Turkish elite.

Husseinid rulers had numerous difficulties. They could only achieve stability and autonomy from the Ottoman sultan by getting the support of the Turkish elite and the Janissaries. Trade and foreign relations were developed, but economic and security problems increased spending. Tunisia's wealth was also used for the beys' private spending, and taxes from one-third of the population was not collected because the army was afraid to travel to the remote regions where the Berbers lived.

WHEN A TURK IS NOT A TURK

The Ottomans went into an informal partnership with pirates to gain naval supremacy in the Mediterranean. Piracy brought handsome profits from raids on ships and coastal towns, and from the ransoming or sale of hostages. Many of the pirates were European and the Turks could not count on their loyalty. Eventually the "Turks by profession" became so wealthy and powerful that they could counter the power of the Turkish military. Trading powers also began to bribe the pirates to ensure safe travel.

Following United States independence, American ships were no longer protected by the British navy, and many American crewmen were captured and enslaved by pirates off the North African coast. In 1800 the United States signed a treaty with the Husseinid bey that promised an annual tribute in return for immunity from attack by Tunisian-based pirates. In 1805 a Tunisian mission to Washington exchanged the tribute for a trade agreement. A joint agreement signed by Britain, France, and Tunisia in 1818 made it illegal to arm pirates or to take Christians as slaves.

Ahmad Bey (1837–55) started a modernization program based on the Western model. He introduced military reform so that Tunisians could be trained to defend their own country and he bought military hardware. A supporter of social reforms, he abolished slavery and outlawed discrimination against Jews. In 1845 the Ottoman ruler finally recognized Tunisian independence.

Tunisia paid dearly for Ahmad Bey's ambitious plans and for the embezzlement of funds by his prime minister, Mustapha Khaznadar. The bankrupt government borrowed heavily from Britain, France, and Italy. These countries, particularly France, sought political mileage out of Tunisia's debt. To reorganize Tunisia's finances, an international financial commission (IFC) was set up in Tunis in 1868, represented by Tunisia, Britain, France, and Italy. Tunisia was stripped of its independence: foreign relations were given up to the Ottoman empire, economic affairs to the IFC, and only internal matters remained under the control of the bey. France had begun its economic domination of Tunisia by establishing French-owned companies to buy land for development. By the time of the French protectorate, French economic control was complete.

Political struggles were common in the 16th and 17th centuries. Bey Murad won a typical struggle in 1631, and started a hereditary line of *bey-pasha*, the title he adopted.

Bey Mohammed as-Sadiq was forced to sign the Bardo Treaty making Tunisia a French protectorate.

THE FRENCH PROTECTORATE

At the Berlin Congress of 1878, the European powers divided Africa among themselves. Britain recognized France's control over Tunisia in return for control over Cyprus. All France needed was an excuse to occupy Tunisia. It came in 1881, when, claiming to be pursuing Tunisian Kroumirie tribesmen who had crossed the border to raid in Algeria, France invaded Tunisia. A force of 36,000 French troops headed for the bey's palace in Tunis, while the French navy seized Bizerte—both far from the scene of the alleged raid.

Power over foreign relations and finance were surrendered to France, who appointed a minister as advisor to the bey. Tunisian uprisings to protest French intervention resulted in France's capture of Sousse, Gafsa, Gabès, and Kairouan. French control over Tunisia was made complete with the signing of the 1883 Convention of La Marsa, a treaty that allowed the dynasty of beys to continue, with the French ruling through them.

MODERNIZATION The treaty gave the French powers to introduce administrative, judicial, and financial reforms. A modernization program followed, along with efficient tax collection. Roads, railways, hospitals, schools, and modern sanitation works were built, and ports improved. The best agricultural land was taken by the French. With their technology and

financial capacity, the French were able to reintroduce the large-scale cultivation of olives and grapes that had existed centuries before. These crops and Tunisia's mineral reserves were tapped for export.

The justice system was reformed with the shariah courts handling only personal matters of marriage and inheritance, while other matters were addressed by the French legal code. Two appeal courts were set up, the first in Algiers, the second in France. French became the official language, and military service was compulsory for Tunisians and French in Tunisia.

A social revolution in Tunisia was brought about by changing the rural society to a commercial and urban one. Land reform created difficulties for both the French and Tunisians. Traditionally land was owned collectively and represented wealth to the Tunisians. First Islamic rules governing land inheritance brought complications, then the French changed communal ownership to individual ownership. Wealth then shifted to those able to work the land most productively. Tunisians had difficulty adjusting to this change since their resources of money, education, and tools were much poorer than their European counterparts. Modernization, it seemed, benefited the elite and not the masses.

French economic intervention laid the infrastructure for Tunisia's future stability.

French attempts to suppress the Neo-Destour party only increased its popularity. Its leader, Bourguiba, was exiled and imprisoned several times in the course of the fight for independence.

THE RISE OF NATIONALISM

In 1890 a small Western-educated group called the Young Tunisians began demanding more reforms and greater Tunisian participation in government. In 1907 they promoted their ideas through their own French language newspaper, *Le Tunisien.* Sheikh Taalbi, one of the leaders of the group, wrote a widely distributed book demanding that reforms be made. This spurred the formation, after World War I, of the Destour (Constitutional) Party. Its members belonged to the conservative elite: men who were well-educated and wealthy. In 1920 the Destour Party called for the reinstatement of the constitution of 1861, with some changes. It was essentially a demand for a constitutional form of government where Tunisians and Europeans would have equal rights.

The French responded with repression, arresting the leader of the Destour Party. The bey threatened to abdicate if the Destour reforms were not accepted, and French troops promptly surrounded his palace. Only minor reforms were conceded. Disillusioned by the failure of the Destour Party, younger middle-class nationalists began a new party, the Neo-Destour (New Constitutional), in 1934. A more aggressive leader was found in Habib Bourguiba, a French-educated Tunisian lawyer.

WORLD WAR II AND INDEPENDENCE

Germany occupied France in World War II, and the Germans fought in Tunisia for six months from November 1942. When the Axis powers were defeated in North Africa in 1943, Tunisia came under the control of the Free French. The Tunisians expected independence as a natural progression from supporting the French in the war, but they were disillusioned. The French deposed the bey and tried to capture Bourguiba, who fled to Egypt in 1945, where he continued his campaign for Tunisian independence.

But realizing that the political climate was changing in the Arab states, the French finally allowed the formation, in 1951, of a government that included some nationalist leaders. When the Tunisians urged a faster pace toward the formation of a parliament, French repression returned. Nationalist groups went underground and popular demonstrations increased, accompanied by sporadic acts of terrorism.

In July 1954 the French promised to guide Tunisia toward independence. Bourguiba, who had been permitted to return in September 1949 only to be confined at the outbreak of rebellion, supervised the convention signed in 1955. The result was limited self-rule. Most Neo-Destour members rejected the offer, but Bourguiba accepted the agreement as a stepping stone to independence. On March 20, 1956, Tunisia was pronounced independent with a constitutional monarchy ruled by the bey. At the first national legislative elections, the Neo-Destour Party won the majority of seats and Habib Bourguiba became president of the National Assembly. In 1957 the Assembly adopted a constitution ending the rule of the beys.

Habib Bourguiba, the first president of the Republic of Tunisia.

AFTER INDEPENDENCE

Bourguiba was reelected president in 1964, 1969, and 1974. In 1975 the constitution was amended to make Bourguiba president-for-life. By 1964 the Neo-Destour Party, renamed Parti Socialiste Destourien (PSD), had become the only legal political organization.

Bourguiba declared Islam the state religion to win the cooperation of the Muslims. He went further, however, and modified the Islamic institutions of education, justice, medical services, and the status of women, to better compete in the modern world. The Code of Personal Status was passed, giving wives the legal power to institute divorce proceedings against their husbands. Polygamy was outlawed, even though Islamic law permits a Muslim man to have up to four wives, and abortion and birth control were legalized. The powers of the shariah courts were neutralized and turned over to the civil courts. Distinctions between religious and public schools were abolished. Women were encouraged to enter all trades and professions. In 1984 two women were included in Bourguiba's cabinet. Opposition from the Islamic fundamentalists grew, in voice and number, leading to riots and plots against the government.

Economic reforms were also introduced, giving the government control of business and services. Foreign-owned land was nationalized, and an agricultural collectivization program begun. (This project eventually failed for lack of support from the rural Tunisians, and the government liberalized the economy.) Development in the 1960s and early 1970s was phenomenal, but declining demand for petroleum from the mid-1970s, coupled with the high cost of reforms, slowed economic growth.

Political repression of an independent labor movement was part of the government's economic strategy. In 1978 rising unemployment and soaring food prices led to opposition from the once loyal trade union movement and students, and widespread protests gave way to riots and a general strike. Violent clashes led to stern government action, leaving 50 dead. About 200 labor officials, including the union leader, were arrested. The unrest forced the government to attempt political reform. The trade union leaders were released from prison, and the one-party system ended, as opposition parties were gradually recognized as legal. Bourguiba formed a new party, the National Front, which won 94.6% of the vote and all 126 seats in the National Assembly. Other political groups claimed electoral fraud. After 1983 more opposition groups were legalized.

The economic slump of 1982–83 led to riots and strikes during which 100 people were killed and trade union leaders were arrested. There was tighter government control and a stiffer rein on the opposition as Bourguiba grew increasingly conservative and paranoid. He reshuffled his cabinet, getting rid of loyal aides and for a while turned even against his wife and son. He dismissed his prime minister and prevented two legal opposition groups from participating in an election.

In 1987 the government rounded up Islamic fundamentalists who were tried by a state security court and found guilty of terrorist activities and plotting against the government. The minister of the interior, General Zine el-Abidine Ben Ali, who conducted this crackdown, was named prime minister by Bourguiba in 1987. In November that year, Ben Ali was sworn in as president after seven doctors declared Bourguiba senile and too ill to rule.

In many countries with a Muslim majority, Islam governs all personal, social, and political aspects of life. Bourguiba's reforms upset this traditional order, particularly issues concerning women and the family.

41

GOVERNMENT

ACCORDING TO THE CONSTITUTION OF 1959 Tunisia's state religion is Islam, but the government is a secular (nonreligious) one. Since the days of Bourguiba's presidency, groups with a political agenda based on Islam have been illegal. One reason for this is the strong influence of popular Islam, a religion combining Islamic values and folk beliefs. Such a religion runs contrary to the original Islamic teachings, and is preached to the poor and uneducated in rural areas.

GOVERNMENT LEADERS

Executive power lies with the president, who is head of state, head of the government, and commander-in-chief of the army. He or she must be a Muslim, a Tunisian citizen born of a Tunisian father and grandfather, and at least 40 years old.

The president is elected by the people every five years and cannot be elected for more than two consecutive five-year terms. Besides formulating and directing state policy, the president appoints judges, provincial governors, high-ranking officials such as the mayor of Tunis, and the cabinet (council of ministers). Since 1969 the cabinet has been headed by a prime minister, who reports to the president. The prime minister assumes the responsibilities of the president in the case of death or disability.

Legislative power lies with the chamber of deputies, which has 163 members elected for a five-year term. The president has to sign all bills put forward by the chamber before they can become law, but the president's decision can be overridden by a two-thirds majority in the chamber. Since the chamber is in session only twice a year, the president can issue decrees that have the force of law during an emergency if the chamber is in recess.

The voting age is 20 years and above. Political candidates must be at least 30 years old and born of a Tunisian father.

In 1987 a new cabinet was formed that excluded Bourguiba loyalists. President Zine el-Abidine Ben Ali promised to amend the constitution and liberalize politics. There was to be freedom of the press. In the first year of his presidency he released 8,000 political and nonpolitical prisoners condemned by the Bourguiba regime. The state security courts were abolished.

Opposite: **The headquarters of the ruling party, Rassemblement Constitutionnel Democratique (RCD), is at Place de la Kasbah.**

President Ben Ali.

RECENT POLITICAL EVENTS

President Ben Ali changed the ruling party's name to Rassemblement Constitutionnel Democratique (RCD) to reflect its commitment to democratic reform. In 1988 a multiparty system was introduced and the office of president-for-life was abolished. In the 1989 elections Ben Ali was the only candidate for the office of president. His party won 80% of the legislative votes. Members of the illegal and extremist Islamic fundamentalist party, Mouvement de la Tendance Islamique (MTI), renamed Hizb an-Nahdah, ran as independents and won 13% of the vote.

After an attack on the RCD headquarters, the government began a crackdown on the Islamic fundamentalists, particularly Hizb an-Nahdah. Following the discovery of explosives alleged to be for terrorist activities, thousands of Hizb an-Nahdah's members and senior officials were arrested by December 1990. This crackdown provoked demonstrations by Islamic militants that led to widely supported pro-Iraqi demonstrations in early 1991, following the outbreak of the Gulf War between Iraq and the US-led multinational force.

After the 1994 election, opposition groups occupied 19 out of 163 seats. But the government is still concerned with the Islamic fundamentalist threat, which has worsened Tunisia's ties with some Western countries and neighboring Arab ones; the government believes these countries are harboring the fundamentalists. Tunisia's situation is tense as the majority of the people seem to favor Iraq's version of Islamic

النظام العام محمد دبيش VXB170

fundamentalism and Saddam Hussein is a folk hero. It is difficult to predict how long the government's tight rein over the opposition will be able to control the situation when new radical groups are continually being formed, some with the reported aim of armed revolt.

LOCAL GOVERNMENT

Tunisia is divided into 23 governorates, each named after its chief town. This decentralization of power, which gives the people a more active role in government, was realized after 1987 when Ben Ali took over from Bourguiba's 30-year-old rule of Tunisia.

A governorate is headed by a governor appointed by the president. The governor is assisted by elected municipal councils and a council of members nominated by the governor for a three-year term. A governorate is subdivided into delegations, the number of which depends on the size of the province and its social and economic importance. Each delegation is then subdivided into municipalities or communes.

Riot police in Tunis keep the peace in armored tanks. The path toward achieving Ben Ali's promise of multiparty representation in government and freedom of the press has been strewn with opposition allegations of election fraud, arrests of Islamic fundamentalists, censorship of publications sympathetic to the fundamentalist cause, and accusations by Amnesty International of human rights violations in the treatment of political prisoners, especially Islamic fundamentalists.

Tunisia's Code of Personal Status has altered the role of women, giving them increased opportunities of employment and control over their lives.

SYSTEMS OF JUSTICE

The 1959 constitution replaced shariah (Islamic) and rabbinical (Jewish) courts with civil courts. Magistrates are appointed by the president upon recommendations of the Supreme Council of Magistracy. Every accused person is considered innocent until proven guilty and guaranteed the right to a lawyer, who is court-appointed if necessary. The high court hears cases of high treason such as acts against state security, abuse of public authority, and intentionally misleading the head of state to damage national interest. High court judges are selected by the chamber of deputies.

Civil and criminal law is patterned on French law. The Higher Council of the Judiciary acts as the judicial watchdog to keep the justice system independent of political influences.

HIERARCHY OF COURTS There are cantonal courts (51), courts of first instance (13), courts of appeal (6), a court of final appeal, a high court, a council of state, and a military tribunal. Cantonal courts are for petty and misdemeanor charges. One magistrate rules over these cases. A court of first instance has four chambers: civil and commercial, personal status, correctional, and social. A panel of three judges presides.

A court of appeal has four chambers: civil, correctional, accusation, and criminal. The court of final appeal in Tunis has three civil and commercial chambers and one criminal chamber. Appeals from the lower courts arrive here and are reviewed by a panel of three judges.

SHARIAH AND RABBINICAL COURTS

Shariah law is derived from many sources: the Koran, the teachings of Prophet Mohammed, and the interpretations of Islamic legal experts. In shariah courts Muslim judges rule according to shariah law. Prior to the French protectorate, shariah law was applied to all Tunisians and in all situations, the only exception being Jews. The large Jewish community had its own rabbinical courts, based on Jewish law, which dealt with disputes over personal status, family matters, and succession—all other matters were ruled by the shariah courts according to Islamic law.

During the French protectorate, shariah courts existed with limited powers. They ruled only in cases of marriage, divorce, inheritance, and land ownership. A secular court system to cover criminal and commercial matters was created for all Tunisians.

After independence, shariah courts were abolished and the Code of Personal Status was adopted for all Muslims. In 1957 it applied to all Tunisians, and rabbinical courts were abolished.

CODE OF PERSONAL STATUS

This code altered the legal basis for the family and the status of women, not by rejecting Islamic values but rather by modernizing the principles. To many Muslims, however, any alteration is considered blasphemous.

In Tunisia, as in other Arab countries, a paternalistic society is an important part of tradition. According to tradition, men were the heads of households—the decision makers and judges, hearing disputes between family members and deciding on punishment. Men inherited property, were educated to the highest affordable level, and took jobs outside the home. Women were protected by but subordinate to men. The traditional social unit was the extended family, usually living in one house, with the head being the oldest male. Property was held in common by the family. Men worked together and expenses were divided equally. Women looked after all children until the age of 6 when boys came under the care of their father, who made all decisions concerning their education and discipline. Girls remained under the care of their mothers until marriage. Muslim men were allowed up to four wives and had the power to divorce a wife by saying "I divorce thee" three times in front of male witnesses.

When the Code of Personal Status was passed, the way in which family matters were settled changed. Polygamy was outlawed and divorce became a court decision, not a man's personal one. Either marriage partner could petition for divorce. The legal age for marriage was set in 1964 at 17 years for females and 20 for males. The mother had guardianship of all young children in a divorce, but the court had the power to appoint a guardian where a mother was deemed unfit. All women were encouraged to reach the highest educational and professional levels within their capability. They were given a choice and a voice when abortion and contraceptives were legalized and when they got the right to vote.

DEFENSE AND FOREIGN RELATIONS

Tunisia has an army, a navy, and an air force. Twelve months' military service is compulsory for men. There is also a national police force, known as the Public Order Brigade, and a national guard.

Tunisia advocates the peaceful settlement of conflicts and dialogue in its relations with foreign powers. It works towards Maghrib, African, and Arab unity. President Ben Ali was the chairman of the Organization of African Unity in 1994–1995. Tunisia's relations with France and the United States are good despite occasional setbacks, such as in 1994 when Tunisia accused these countries of harboring Islamic fundamentalists. France and the United States supply Tunisia with weapons, military training, and economic and technical support.

THE UNION OF ARAB MAGHRIB The Maghrib Consultative Community was formed in Tunis in 1964 with the aim of creating an economic community. In February 1989, at the North African heads of state meeting,

The Bourguiba family mausoleum in Monastir, resting place of the late president. During his term of office, Tunisia came close to signing a treaty with Libya to merge the two countries into an Islamic Arab Republic. This was not realized due to pressure from Algeria and Bourguiba's own government.

48

the Union of the Arab Maghrib (UMA) was formed consisting of Algeria, Libya, Mauritania, Morocco, and Tunisia. The UMA holds regular meetings of ministers of foreign affairs and works toward the removal of barriers to the free movement of goods, people, services, and capital in the Maghrib.

In April 1994 the UMA member countries decided on 11 agreements to improve cooperation and trade within the Maghrib. In June 1993 President Ben Ali, in an address to the European Parliament, asked for the formation of a Euro-Maghrib Development Bank. Since then Ben Ali, UMA, and the European Union (EU) have been working toward a closer political and commercial relationship. In July 1995 Tunisia was the first UMA country to sign an agreement of association with the EU. A Euro-Mediterranean conference took place later that year in Barcelona, after a preparatory meeting of 11 countries in Tabarka, Tunisia.

A number of Maghrib institutions have been set up in Tunis, including the Maghrib Bank for Investment and Foreign Trade and the Maghrib Trade Union. To demonstrate Tunisia's focus on Maghrib unity, the post of Secretary of State for Maghrib Affairs was created.

Tunisia is also a member of the Arab League, an organization formed in 1945 by the heads of Arab states to strengthen Arab unity.

ISRAEL AND THE PLO Tunisia supports Palestinian autonomy and a peaceful resolution to the Palestinian problem. When Israel invaded Beirut in 1982, the Palestine Liberation Organization (PLO) was forced to withdraw from Lebanon. Tunisia admitted the PLO chairman and nearly 1,000 Palestinian fighters, and the new PLO headquarters was established in Tunis. A framework for Tunisian-Palestinian cooperation has been created with a large commission to plan joint projects in various fields. A liaison office opened in Gaza in April 1995 and another is planned for Jericho.

Tunisia has been a watchdog in the enforcement of the principles of the Union of the Arab Maghrib. When Libya and Morocco formed an alliance with the potential to create two power blocks in the Maghrib, Tunisia called a meeting of the Maghrib heads of state to rekindle the unification drive and prevent a realignment of power.

ECONOMY

THE PRIVATE SECTOR leads economic growth in Tunisia but the government plays an active role. The government relinquished control of certain industries in 1987, and private companies now produce 60% of the country's output. The economy is diversified with a thriving tourist sector, developing industrial and mining sectors, and a well-established agricultural sector.

The average income for Tunisians has risen from US$30 in 1956 to US$1,900 in 1996. The economy has grown at an annual rate of 5.4% since 1987. Tunisia's foreign debt is US$8.7 billion, of which US$7.4 billion is a long-term development loan. Unemployment has been reduced from 30% in the late 1970s to 15.8% in 1992. Between 1992 and 1995, 226,000 more jobs were created in the manufacturing, agricultural, and service sectors. Developing the people's potential is a priority with the government. The bulk of the national budget goes to education, health care, housing, and social services.

Opposite and left: **Dates, an important Tunisian export, are grown in oases such as this one in Nefta (left).**

An irrigated oasis at Nefta. In 1991, only 2% of arable land was planted with permanent crops, while 8% was irrigated and produced 25% of the total output. Plans are under way for the building of dams, lakes, and catchment basins, and for drilling wells and boreholes to look for new sources of underground water believed to exist in the Saharan region. Forestation of 790,000 acres (320,000 hectares) is also planned to reduce soil erosion.

AGRICULTURE

The agricultural sector provides most of Tunisia's own food and employs a third of the workforce. Cash crops include wheat, barley, grapes, olives, citrus fruit, and dates. Market produce such as tomatoes, sugarbeets, potatoes, artichokes, fruit, and almonds have been added to diversify cultivation and increase income. Tunisia has an early growing season so exports reach Europe ahead of the European season. Cotton is also grown to supply the textile industry, and esparto grass is grown on the steppes.

The government has undertaken irrigation and soil conservation projects to improve production. To raise funds for the agricultural sector, the government created the Agricultural Investment Promotion Agency and the National Agricultural Development Bank. At test farms, researchers experiment on improving the quality and variety of crops. A higher institute of agricultural research and instruction links farmers and researchers. New methods of cultivation and research results are made known to the farmers and their concerns are brought to the researchers to evaluate.

THE OLIVE TREE

Many centuries ago the Romans called El Djem in Tunisia the "olive oil capital." The crop's importance was reestablished by French farmer Paul Bourde in the late 1900s. Bourde offered plots of land around Sfax at a reasonable price, and within a few years people settled to grow olive trees. In 1880 there were 400,000 olive trees in Tunisia; now there are 50 million.

Sfax, the olive oil capital, exports this "Tunisian gold." Olive groves near Sfax stretch for up to 50 miles (80 km) inland from the coast. The olive tree, which is drought-resistant, is well adapted to Tunisia's climate.

Today Tunisia is the world's fourth largest producer of olive oil and the second largest exporting country after Greece. In 1992 olive oil was the largest agricultural export. The Tunisian National Office for Oil supervises the collection, stocking, and export of the oil.

ANIMAL REARING

In the steppes rearing animals is a major occupation. It is carried out on an even larger scale in the north, which has plenty of water and more grazing land. Poultry farming has become popular, as it supplements farmers' income as well as the protein in Tunisians' diet.

FISHING

In 1992 commercial fishing overtook olive oil in export value. There are about 50,000 fishermen in the industry. A government program helps fishermen buy new boats in exchange for regular payments of a portion of the catch. Tunisia exports tuna, sardines, shrimp, and lobster.

FORESTRY

The main export in this sector is cork. The bark of cork oak is first stripped off when the tree is 20 years old. The first layer is rough and is shredded for use in products such as floor tiles and table mats. Every 10 years, bark is removed, the rough surface scraped, and the remaining layer flattened and dried before further processing.

Donkeys, mules, and camels are reared by the nomads in the Saharan regions where they are useful for transporting people and goods. These animals also help in plowing and moving machinery. Here a camel is turning a wheel to crush olives to extract oil. There are more than 2,000 olive presses in Sfax.

MINING

Tunisia is rich in mineral wealth but its exploitation is a relatively new industry. Until recently the main substance mined was phosphate. It has been overtaken by petroleum as the most profitable mineral. Other substances mined are gas, iron ore, lead, zinc, uranium, barite, limestone, gypsum, silver, fluorspar, and marine salt. Tunisia is the fourth largest producer of phosphate with 5% of the world's reserves.

Oil exploration in Tunisia began in 1956 after reserves were found in Algeria. In 1992 it was estimated that reserves of 1.7 billion barrels remained, sufficient to maintain production at 1992 levels for another 43.5 years. Total production in 1992 contributed to 15% of total export

Phosphate plant in Met-laoui. Phosphate and its by-products account for 9.6% of Tunisia's export earnings. Phosphate is mined in the Gafsa and Kef regions and trans-ported to chemical plants in Sfax, Maknassy, and Gabès, where it is made into sulfuric acid, nitrates, and fertilizers.

earnings. The government controls 50% of Tunisia's oil industry. With the help of foreign investments, the Skhira and Bizerte petroleum ports were developed. The first refinery at Bizerte has been completed and the second is due to be built soon.

Natural gas deposits were discovered in the south and off the Kerkenna Islands. Gas production, however, does not meet local demand, so pipelines from these sources connect with the Italian-Algerian pipeline to supply the Tunisian industrial sector.

INDUSTRY

In 1993 manufacturing accounted for 38.5% of export earnings. Heavy industry, developed with the help of foreign investments, focuses on mineral refining. Oil refineries, chemical plants (producing phosphate fertilizers), iron and steelworks, and cement works have grown around the sites of deposits. Auto assembly plants put together mainly trucks and tractors.

Oil exploration offshore. Of the 22 oilwells drilled in 1992, seven were offshore.

Tunisia's light industries include food processing (flour milling, food canning, sugar refining, and olive oil processing), textile and leather production, and paper and wood processing. European clothing firms have subcontracted work to Tunisian factories because of the low wages and high skills of the labor force. Recently textiles and clothing have become the top export. The other burgeoning industry is electronics. Cooperative-run, small cottage industries produce traditional crafts. Mostly handmade using antique tools, these crafts have a long history in Tunisia.

TOURISM

Tourism is a very important source of revenue; in 1994, it earned US$1.3 billion. Income from tourism offsets 60% of Tunisia's trade deficit.

The government has made the development of this sector a priority and deals harshly with Islamic fundamentalists who target tourist sites for terrorist attacks. Tourists are being encouraged to move away from the beaches to explore the cultural centers inland and more exotic locations in the Sahara.

The public and private sectors work closely to keep the tourism machinery running smoothly. The Ministry of Tourism and the Office National du Tourisme Tunisien (ONTT) are responsible for promoting and publicizing tourist sites and maintaining historical buildings; the private sector develops hotels and support services.

Tourists arrive through six international airports and five passenger ports. The national airline, Tunisair, is owned by the Tunisian Government (51%), Air France, and Tunisian citizens. Tuninter offers domestic flights.

TRADE

Tunisia exports minerals (mainly phosphates and petroleum), agricultural products (olive oil and market produce), textiles and clothing, and chemicals (fertilizers). It imports mainly consumer goods (food, live animals, and textiles), raw and processed materials (iron and steel), and agricultural and industrial equipment.

Major trading partners are France, Italy, Germany, and the United States. In 1994 the Union of Arab Maghrib (UAM) agreed to establish a free

Hot spring in Cape Bon. Tunisia is a popular tourist spot, ahead of Morocco, Egypt, Kenya, and Senegal in Africa. To encourage European and American tourists, Tunisia waives the requirement of a visa. Tunisia's popularity with tourists is due to a combination of its culture, rich historic and artistic past, and Mediterranean climate in the north, with an abundance of beautiful beaches.

trade zone. In the same year Tunisia entered into an agreement with the EU to align its economy with that of the EU. The process is to be developed over 12 years. Tunisia could then supply the EU market while developing self-sufficiency within the Maghrib states, a ready source of cheaper goods free of tax. Between 1992 and 1995, exports increased by 7.2%.

Crafts exported include carpets, blankets, leather goods, pottery, basketry, and brass and olive-wood utensils. They are popular with Tunisians and tourists alike. This shop specializes in drums.

FOREIGN INVESTMENT

Tunisia's thriving economy, strategic location (surrounded by Europe, Africa, and the Middle East), and investment benefits attract investors from the Arab states, the EU countries, Japan, and the United States. More than 1,800 firms have joint ventures or direct investments in Tunisian companies.

Investment laws passed in 1972 and amended in 1974 and 1989 have the aim of maximizing export potential while developing consumer goods (including food) to minimize imports. Benefits are given to encourage manufacturing, especially of textiles, for export and industrial production in underdeveloped areas for the local market.

TRANSPORTATION

A comprehensive transportation network connects production sites with ports and cities, providing efficient distribution of goods to the local population and for export.

LAND Inexpensive bus services operate in the cities, but timetables and routes are complicated and tickets must be bought at the relevant office before travel. A fast and reasonably cheap way to travel is by taxi. For travel between cities and outlying towns the *louage* ("loo-AHJ") is a good alternative to train travel, which is limited to certain areas. *Louages* are shared taxis that have a fixed fare and take up to five passengers. They leave from their departure points when the quota is filled or the driver decides that no more passengers are likely to appear.

Railways are maintained by the Tunisian National Railway Company, and the 1,400-mile (2,250-km) network serves two-thirds of the country in mainly the northern and central regions. Trains transport about 30 million travelers and 11 million tons (10 million tonnes) of freight yearly. An underground service connects Tunis to the suburbs including major institutions like the university just outside Tunis.

AIR People arrive through six international airports—Tunis-Carthage, Monastir-Skanés, Djerba-Mellita, Tozeur, Sfax, and Tabarka.

PORTS The five major commercial seaports are Tunis-La Goulette-Radés, Sfax, Bizerte, Gabès, and Sousse.

COMMUNICATIONS

PHONE AND POSTAL SERVICE The postal and telephone system is modern and efficient. Stamps are sold at Tunisian post offices, known as Poste Téléphone Télégraph (PTT), tobacco shops, and newspaper stands. Public telephones are found in cubicles in small windowless and doorless shops along most main streets, and can be used only during opening hours. Businesses generally have facsimile machines and modems hooked up to their computers. A 24-hour courier service is supplied through Rapide Poste International at the Tunis-Carthage Airport.

TELEVISION A government-controlled television station broadcasts in Arabic and French.

NEWSPAPERS There are daily and weekly papers. In 1996 three out of five daily papers were published in French.

Telephone and fax services are conveniently located in Tunisian cities. Attendants on duty provide change.

TUNISIANS

TUNISIANS ARE A multicultural blend of peoples. Highly tolerant of religious and ethnic differences, Tunisia is progressive compared to some Arab states. Tunisian women are relatively free to pursue educational and professional goals. There are rich, business-suited, pro-Western Tunisians and robed, uneducated herders, who are suspicious of Western values and barely survive off the land. What unites them is Islam, hard work, the desire to progress, tolerance, and generosity of spirit.

POPULATION STATISTICS

The 1994 census recorded the population at 8,882,000. Population density is far greater than that of Algeria or Libya. The Tunisian population is expected to grow by 2.2% a year, to reach 10 million by the year 2000. This rate of growth, considered high by international standards, is one of the lowest among African countries.

Opposite and left: **Shepherds near Maktar, a village in the Dorsale mountains near Tunis, and children in Sousse. Rural people have fewer opportunities to improve their livelihood.**

The population density is 140 people per square mile (54 per square km), but the population is not distributed evenly. In the Saharan region, it is as low as 9 people per square mile (5 per square km). About 60% of the population live in urban centers, which total 20% of the land. (In Tunis alone there are 1 million people.) The remaining people, mainly farmers and herders, live in the northeast, the Sahel, the steppes, and the Saharan region.

Since independence in 1957, improved public health care has increased average life expectancy from 50 to approximately 71 years. Infant mortality is 32 per 1,000 births. There are publicly and privately financed programs to assist poor and disadvantaged people.

Tunisia has a very young population, with 68% being under 30 years old and 56% under 15.

The adult literacy rate in 1990 was 65.3% (men, 74.2%; women, 56.3%), up by 35% since independence in 1957. Education is highly prized and seen as the only way out of poverty and into a higher social class.

MIGRATION AND DISTRIBUTION

The urban centers generally have better job opportunities and facilities such as schools and hospitals. Consequently, there has been a constant movement of people from rural to urban centers, creating a serious problem in Tunisia.

The government tried resettling nomads and semi-nomads in permanent villages and teaching them to grow crops for export, but they preferred to seek employment abroad. In the 1990s, 350,000 Tunisians were working in France and Libya, and they usually sent money home. In 1989 the money remitted from abroad totalled 5% of Tunisia's Gross National Product. In 1990, 207,500 Tunisians lived and worked in France alone.

Lack of modern conveniences has caused a heavy migration of Tunisians to cities and abroad, leaving a population of older people in rural regions.

ETHNIC GROUPS

The racial blend of Tunisians is the result of the original Berber stock mixing with Phoenicians, Romans, Spaniards, Arabs, and the French. There are also very small groups of Europeans, Africans, Jews, and Spaniards.

ARAB-BERBERS The Arabs came to Tunisia in the 7th century with the intention of conquering the Berbers and spreading Islam. Many of them settled down and married the Berbers, spreading Arab language and culture and creating a new Maghrib identity. Arabization was complete by the 11th century following the invasion of a few thousand Beni Hillal Bedouin who converted a few million Berbers to Islam. The Arabs were generally of slender build with dark hair, eyes, and skin.

BERBERS Now only 3% of the population, much less than in Algeria or Morocco, today's Berbers are descendants of those who retained their identity by evading successive invading groups. The majority settled in the Atlas Mountains, the Sahara, and on Djerba Island where they followed a nomadic life introduced by the Beni Hillal Bedouin tribes. Today many Berbers still raise herds of sheep and goats and live in caves, mud-walled homes, and underground homes in Matmata, Médenine, and Tataouine, all towns in the Ksour region.

Young, single Berber men leave their homes for cities and even emigrate to France and Libya in search of work and higher wages to send home. They usually return to look for a wife. Berber villages are populated

Above and opposite: **The majority of Tunisians are Arab-Berber, with some African and European influences. A lighter-colored skin generally indicates European or Berber stock.**

by the old and dying, many of whom are women who struggle to eke out a living by weaving carpets.

The Berbers are the first known inhabitants of the Maghrib and are believed to have lived there for thousands of years before the arrival of the Phoenicians. Their origin is mysterious. It is believed that they evolved from a combination of peoples: Libyan, Egyptian, Persian, Phoenician, Italian, and Iberian. Generally stocky in build, having light hair and blue eyes, Berbers are independent and individualistic.

Some scholars believe that "Berber" is not the original name of these people as it is a derogatory word that comes from the Greek *barabaroi* or Arabian *brabra*, used to describe strangers whose language is unintelligible.

AFRICANS This minority group are descendants of Africans who were brought to Tunisia as domestic slaves and concubines. They affected the population very slightly.

SPANISH Muslims fled from Spain for a few hundred years starting in the 13th century when the Spanish fought to get their territory back from the Ottoman Turks. In Tunisia they intermarried with the local people and left a social and cultural impact on coastal society.

JEWS Jews have been present in Tunisia for almost two thousand years, and today they are mostly merchants and skilled craftspeople. The population of Jews was sufficiently large before independence to require the establishment of rabbinical courts to settle their legal affairs based on religious principles. Several thousand Jews left Tunisia gradually, over two

A rabbi leads in a musical session at the Ghriba Synagogue on Djerba Island. Tunisian Jews live mainly in Tunis, Zarzis (a southern coastal town), and on Djerba Island.

decades, after World War II. The first Jews arrived in Tunisia after Jerusalem was burned by the Roman Emperor Titus. Others came when they were expelled from Spain by the Christian King Philip III. The Jews who came in the early 20th century were middle-class tradespeople from Europe. Tension in the Middle East since independence led to demonstrations against the Jews of Tunisia. The demonstrations and vandalism of synagogues have given rise to feelings of insecurity among the Jews.

EUROPEANS When the French protectorate was established, French and Italians flooded into Tunisia. Generally, the French were the well-to-do elite, while the Italians were mostly working-class people from southern Italy, particularly Sicily. After independence, in the late 1950s and 1960s, the Europeans left in large numbers. The French, especially, left their mark on Tunisia, in the architecture, food, language, tree-lined avenues, sidewalk cafés, and Western clothing, which is worn everywhere. Today, small European communities can be found in Tunis and Bizerte.

CLASS STRUCTURE AND ATTITUDES

The upper middle class of Tunisia—the economic and political elite—are the old aristocratic families, Western-educated civil servants, political leaders, prominent businesspeople, and large landowners. The lower middle class—a quickly growing group—are low-level civil servants, schoolteachers, small business proprietors, skilled service and industrial workers, and independent farmers. The working class are subsistence farmers and agricultural workers. The day laborers, unemployed, and underemployed found in rural areas and shantytowns near urban centers belong to Tunisia's lowest social class.

There is a fundamental difference in attitude between people in fertile northern and coastal Tunisia and those in the more remote central and southern parts. In the fertile areas, people are richer and more in control

Urban people have an essentially Arab outlook but are pro-West, favoring Western institutions and values. They are especially drawn to French culture and lifestyle.

of their lives. They value education, political leadership, commercial success, and wealth. They have a greater sense of security and are aware of their right to property. In the arid regions, people have a sense of helplessness and dependence on God since extremes of climate can affect their livelihood.

Education is of great importance to most Tunisians, but it is the tie that binds among the elite, who are educated at French secondary schools. For higher education many go abroad or to the University of Tunis. The working and lower classes are more in tune with the Arab world and Islam, and less receptive to Westernization. These people make up the majority of the population and the government depends on them for stability. The government walks a tightrope of trying to stay modern and viable in order to keep up with international progress, yet maintaining its Islamic identity. When the Gulf War erupted, for example, the Tunisian government had to publicly denounce the US-led multinational force in Kuwait because the majority of Tunisians supported Saddam Hussein. Farmers and nomads in the rural areas are generally suspicious of things connected with urban life.

In general, Tunisians are warm and generous. They have a civic spirit and very readily lend a hand without thought of reward. Foreigners are pleasantly surprised when Tunisians go out of their way to help them. It is also common to see Tunisians giving alms to the less fortunate, and perhaps this is why beggars are less evident here than in some other North African countries.

Nomads are less attracted to education than urban dwellers because textbook learning cannot prepare them for the harsh realities of living in the fields and deserts.

DRESS

As in most other Islamic countries, traditional Tunisian clothes are mostly loose-fitting robes that cover arms, legs, and heads. In cities, people dress in both Western and traditional clothes, but those wearing Western clothes observe the basic rule of modesty. Many Western-educated and young Tunisians as well as businesspeople prefer Western attire, sometimes complemented with a traditional Tunisian garment like a hat or a loose robe worn as an outer garment for going outdoors.

The *chebias* ("shair-HI-ah," hats) the men wear are tall and brimless. They can be round or flat-topped, brown or red. The color indicates the area they come from. The *djellaba* ("shjuh-LAH-buh") or loose robe is sometimes calf- or ankle-length and long-sleeved. In the desert, men wear a length of fabric tied around their heads like a turban and an extremely loose tunic that can be wrapped around their heads and bodies when they need to protect themselves from the cold, heat, wind, or dust.

Traditional women line their eyes with black kohl, while Berber women have blue dots tattooed on their forehead, nose, and chin. Traditional attire for women is the *sifsari* ("sif-SAH-ri") and *haik* ("hake"), a long tunic and a large sheet that can be pulled over the head and the corners clenched by teeth. The *haik* does double duty as a veil and a wrap to carry packages and babies.

Covering up is the rule, for too much exposed skin is associated with loose morals.

LIFESTYLE

THE GOVERNMENT MAKES a great effort to improve the life of Tunisians living in the more remote parts of the country by providing free education, public housing, traveling libraries, and by promoting traditional crafts, agriculture, fishing, and animal husbandry.

HOUSING

A survey in 1984 found that 71% of all homes in Tunisia were traditional structures, 14% were villas or detached homes belonging mainly to the rich, 9% were squatter dwellings, and 5% were apartments. Though not very popular, high-rise living is being encouraged to maximize the limited land space in major cities.

IN THE CITIES AND TOWNS The movement of large numbers of people from rural areas to the cities in search of work led to the growth of squatter villages or *gourbvilles* just outside the cities. A green belt is being

Opposite: **A brief exchange outside a souk, or shopping area.**

Left: **The government provides public housing for workers.**

Opposite: **Troglodyte homes are dug about 6 feet (2 m) into the earth because long ago the people found it easier to dig through the soft rock than to make bricks out of it. The temperature indoors is consistently cool in the summer and warm in the winter.**

Below: **Traditional homes look impenetrable from the outside, but there is much beauty, and even grandeur, behind the walls.**

established around urban centers to improve air quality and to deter the formation of squatter villages. Trade unions provide housing for members and needy homeowners can apply for help from the national housing fund. Rent is controlled by the government to keep it affordable.

Traditional homes vary widely, but in general, many of them are small and line narrow streets, facing each other. The exterior walls of the houses are painted a universal color. Doors may be painted in different colors, but blue is favored. There are usually three stories, with access from the third story to a flat, livable roof. Rarely are there windows in the exterior walls of Tunisian houses, but courtyards, sometimes with fountains and gardens, are often hidden behind these walls.

IN THE COUNTRYSIDE Farmhouses are roughly made and usually whitewashed. A low wall surrounds the house to keep out stray animals and windblown sand. Their unusual loaf-shaped roofs, which are made entirely of bricks, allow air to circulate more efficiently inside, keeping the house cool in the summer and warm in the winter.

Furnishings are meager and basic. The oven is a brick hole in the wall and one charcoal burner serves as the stove. Refrigeration is nonexistent. Carpets are stored folded then spread out when needed on dirt or stone floors—people sit, sleep, eat, and entertain on carpets.

Water is collected from a communal well some distance away, so frequent trips must be made to keep rural homes supplied with water for cooking, cleaning, and drinking.

IN THE SOUTH AND DESERT AREAS The Tunisian south has some of the most unusual homes, which are occupied by mountain dwellers and nomads. These creative homes have existed for centuries, safeguarding people from extremes of heat and cold, sand, wind, and wild animals.

Nomads carry their tented homes with them on the backs of camels. Bedouin tents are usually made of sacking woven and sewn together by the women. Rugs and blankets complete the furnishings. These broad and low tents house entire families.

Underground dwellings called troglodyte homes, located near Matmata, Médenine, and Chenini are a major tourist attraction. These Berber villages look like the surface of the moon, with craters emitting spirals of smoke. So strange is their appearance that Steven Spielberg filmed *Raiders of the Lost Ark* and *Star Wars* in Matmata.

Troglodyte homes have open courtyards. Rooms, usually four (one each for eating, sleeping, stabling, and storage), radiate out from the courtyard. The storage room holds necessities such as grain, olives, and

animal fodder that can be restocked via a narrow pipe leading to the outside through the ceiling. A tunnel, lined with places for storing tools and other things, connects the various rooms. A gently inclined entrance tunnel, big enough to lead a large animal through, connects the surface with the underground home. A few larger troglodyte homes in Matmata have been converted into hotels.

Farming in the desert climate was difficult and it was possible to have only one good grain crop every few years, so it was vital to defend the village granary—called *ghorfa* ("GHOR-fa," Arabic for room) or *ksar* ("SAHR," Arabic for "fortress")—from attack. Ksars and ghorfas are traditional mud and stone buildings. They were built on flat ridges or in sheltered valleys difficult for strangers to penetrate without being seen from lookout posts. The buildings have several rooms, built side by side and piled up to five or six levels high, linked by interior or exterior stairs, and were built for defense against Arab troops. Grain is now stored nearer the fields, and these old buildings have been converted into homes.

EDUCATION

Most schools in Tunisia are government schools, and private schools (mostly Islamic and Catholic) are subject to government regulation. The curricula applies to all schools to ensure uniformity. A Ministry of National Education formulates and implements educational policy and supervises the standard of teaching and of facilities in primary and secondary schools. Higher education is supervised by the Ministry of Higher Education and Scientific Research.

In 1996 education received 20% of the government's annual budget as it was seen as the main way to social and economic change for individuals and the country. Public education is free from primary to university level, compulsory until the age of 16, and is available to all regardless of gender, class, or ethnic background.

The educational system has three levels: primary school (six years), secondary school (three years), and university (four years) or vocational training (three years). Primary and secondary schools are open six days a week for nine months of the year. Instruction is in Arabic in the early primary school years, then in French. In 1993, 100% of the school-age population was enrolled in primary schools, but the percentage dropped to 44% for secondary school attendance.

Higher education is provided mainly by the University of Tunis (founded in 1960) and its branches in the major cities, and supplemented by university-level advanced schools. Two universities were opened in the 1980s at Monastir and Sfax.

Enrollment for girls is usually a little behind at all levels of education, but generally education, which consumes a quarter of the national budget, promises a better future for the young.

75

A policewoman directs traffic in a Tunis street.

HEALTH AND SOCIAL SECURITY

In the early 1960s, the government introduced a welfare program called the National Social Security Fund, to which employers and employees make contributions. The fund provides benefits for sickness, maternity, family allowances, disability, life insurance, and old age. Social security care for the aged, orphaned, and needy are the responsibility of regional committees.

The government started a family planning program in 1964, the first of its kind in Africa. By 1993 the birth rate had dropped from seven to three children per woman.

WOMEN

Women in Tunisia are freer and more independent than in the other North African and Middle Eastern Islamic states. Habib Bourguiba, the first president, liberated women from subordination to men by creating the Code of Personal Status. Women are encouraged to enter all levels of education and professional life. Their civil rights respecting ownership of property, inheritance, custody of children, and divorce equal those of men.

POLITICAL RIGHTS Women have the right to vote. In 1956 the National Union of Tunisian Women was formed to voice women's problems and aspirations, and to promote female participation in the country's social and political life. Women's concerns regarding health, literacy, employment, and family planning are heard though this organization, which also helps

women cope better personally and professionally by providing courses in literacy, civics, hygiene, family planning, and sewing, among others.

Despite the many safeguards and avenues the government provides to help women advance, old traditions and cultural expectations are obstacles to achieving total independence.

In general, upper- and middle-class women are more daring in experimenting with their newfound liberty than the lower classes and particularly rural women. Today women are not only teachers, seamstresses, and factory or agricultural workers, but lawyers, doctors, politicians, and civil servants. The number of females in schools and the work place does not yet equal that of men, but the number is increasing.

In 1971 there were 83 women town councilors and four women in the Chamber of Deputies. In 1985 there were two women in the cabinet— a minister of public health and a minister of family and women's advancement.

A Berber woman with her baby. Women in rural areas are more likely to accept a traditional role than their sisters in the cities.

RITES OF PASSAGE

Most life-cycle celebrations in Tunisia, regardless of religion, are practiced with a mixture of folklore and rituals. Belief in the evil eye and in evil spirits (djinns) is widespread and very much a part of all celebrations. Since 98% of the population is Muslim, the main life events are observed according to Islamic belief.

BIRTH Seven days after the birth of a child, amulets adorned with fish, coins, or teeth are worn by the child to protect it from evil forces. These amulets are believed to bring good luck.

CIRCUMCISION At 5 or 7 years of age, a boy makes his first visit to the mosque, where he is circumcised by a doctor or a barber. At the precise moment of circumcision, other children break a jar of candy to detract the evil spirits or djinns from entering the boy through the wound.

WEDDINGS Marriage now requires the consent of the woman, who has to be at least 17 years old. It is also now possible for Muslim women to marry outside their faith.

Polygamy is illegal. Women can also initiate divorce proceedings that now must go through a civil court. These legally enforced changes make men socially and psychologically more committed to a marriage contract. Many couples these days protect their interests by having legal documents drawn up stating the terms of marriage and divorce, including the settlement of the dowry. The dowry, which is given by the bride's family, is her "insurance" against a rainy day, and not the price given to the groom for marrying her.

The Islamic bride is treated to full-body treatments in which all bodily hair is waxed off and her skin rubbed with herbs. Her hands and feet are intricately decorated with henna, a natural brown dye.

A traditional week-long or modern two-day celebration is launched with a motorcade of honking, decorated cars. The bride and groom are royally dressed and seated on a dais for family and friends to admire. Men and women go to separate areas to enjoy the wedding dinner.

When everyone has eaten, the bride walks around her father's house seven times to bid farewell before going to start a new life with her husband. Meanwhile the groom is taken out on the town by friends and then left at his door before bedtime. Virginity until marriage, particularly for women, is still prized.

DEATH Wherever possible, Muslim funeral takes place the same day as the death. Female relatives and friends cleanse and dress the body for burial. Male mourners and friends carry the body on a bier to the cemetery, led by a man reading the Koran. Islamic headstones are very simple structures.

Above: **Newlyweds pose for the camera with a family member.**

Opposite: **Two little boys, looking slightly apprehensive, visit a mosque dressed for circumcision.**

Sales staff at a store in Sousse enjoying a moment of camaraderie.

LABOR

Working conditions of workers are safeguarded by the 1966 Labor Code: this includes minimum wage rates for the different occupations, a six-day work week for agricultural workers, and a five-day week of 40–48 hours for all other workers. The code stipulates an annual paid vacation of up to 18 working days, and maternity leave of four to six weeks.

The Agricultural Labor Code grants severance pay, wage increments, and bonuses to farm workers based on harvest size, skill, and seniority. One-third of the labor force is in the agricultural sector, and these benefits reward them for greater production while taking care of their needs.

WORK ATTITUDES

THE IMPORTANCE OF KINSHIP Generally speaking, Tunisians prefer not to work in hierarchical and authoritarian settings. They believe paid employment for its own sake is undignified. Self-respect, independence,

BUSINESS HOURS

Business hours in cities depend on the place of work. Government and public sector offices are open all day, Mondays to Thursdays, except for a two-hour midday break, and half a day on Fridays and Saturdays. Banks are open Mondays to Fridays except for a two-hour midday break. In the summer, offices open very early, many at 7:30 a.m., and close in the early afternoon at about 1:30 p.m. This allows people to enjoy the longer summer daylight hours.

Shopkeepers and taxi drivers also observe a two-hour midday break. During the month of Ramadan (a variable month, following an Islamic calendar), when Muslims fast from sunrise to sunset, shopkeepers close promptly at sunset to observe the daily prayer and the breaking of the fast. Many, however, reopen their shops in the evening, as during the fasting month Muslims stock up for the festival at the end of Ramadan.

Tunisians are used to a paternalistic social structure, which is a feature of Islam, and prefer a sense of community at work to an impersonal and hierarchical business environment.

and pride are greatly prized. Materialism is not a Tunisian characteristic, and good interpersonal ties are more effective than money and status in motivating workers to excel.

The Tunisian management style is to show concern for workers, build teamwork, and make everyone equally responsible for productivity. Workers are encouraged to help each other. Differences in status are blurred and learning is promoted.

Kinship ties—determined by people from the same family, region, village, or school—bring immediate loyalty. Blood and clan ties are always more important than mere friendship. This goes back to the days when a clan lived in a village together and looked out for each other.

BUSINESS ETIQUETTE Generally speaking, Tunisians follow the business etiquette of the French. Upon meeting, people shake hands and exchange business cards that are usually in French, the language of business in Tunisia. Meetings over lunch and dinner or even on weekends are acceptable. Many Tunisian men are not attuned to the relatively new idea of equality and do not bring their wives to business functions. They usually do not discuss their families or personal affairs with business associates.

RELIGION

MUSLIMS MAKE UP 98% of the population and Islam pervades all aspects of social, cultural, and ethical life. Religious freedom is practiced. Most Tunisians are Sunni Muslim, but there are small groups of Kharijites and the mystical Sufis. Christians, mostly French and Italian Roman Catholics, are one percent of the population. Jews also make up only one percent of the population.

ISLAM

The founder of Islam, Mohammed ibn Abdallah (570–632), was orphaned and brought up by relatives in Mecca. At that time Mecca was a center of pagan life where tradesmen made profits from visitors to the pagan shrines. In A.D. 610, Mohammed began receiving revelations from Allah (God) through the angel Gabriel, who taught Mohammed to recite the word of God. This was collected and written in the Koran, the Islamic holy book.

Mohammed—called the Prophet because Muslims believe he is the last in a line of prophets—denounced idol worship, alienating the influential tradesmen. To avoid assassination, he fled to Yathrib (modern Medina in Saudi Arabia) in June 622. Mohammed was invited to be the ruler in Medina. He set up a theocratic state with moral and legal codes for his people, then fought the Meccans and defeated them. Islam spread rapidly from then on as followers traveled far and wide conquering lands to spread the religion. By A.D. 630, two years before Mohammed's death, Islam had spread through all of Arabia. By A.D. 670, it reached Kairouan in Tunisia through Uqba ibn Nafi.

Above: **Muslim women in Tunisia wear white *haik*, the cover-all cloth. Sometimes they clench it in their teeth to hold it up.**

Opposite: **A Muslim waits at the door of the Barber's Mosque in Kairouan, shrine of the Prophet's close companion.**

ISLAMIC TEXTS

"Koran" means "recitation," for in reciting it a Muslim feels the poetry of God's word. Mohammed was taught to recite the word of God, and he in turn taught his followers. Since many people were illiterate then, it was the best way to spread the religion. These recitations were collected and written down 18 years after Mohammed's death, in A.D. 650. They are divided into 114 chapters or *surahs*, arranged from the longest to the shortest. Each surah is named. There are four parts to the Koran: worship of Allah, day of judgment, proclamations and stories of earlier prophets (in Islam, Mohammed is the last prophet), and social laws. A set of commands encourage charity, kindness, sobriety, and humility, and prohibit murder, adultery, idolatry, and meanness.

No one is allowed to alter the Koran.

The Hadith, also known as the Sunna, are collected sayings, teachings, and characteristics of the Prophet's personal behavior, recorded by those who knew him. Following the example of the Prophet's life is a prerequisite to being a good Muslim. The Hadith is not an alternative to the Koran. Sunni Muslims recognize the Hadith as a basis of Muslim law. Shi'a Muslims do not.

Interpretations from the Koran and Hadith form the shariah, a legal system guiding the spiritual, ethical, and social life of Muslims. In traditional Islamic countries, civil, criminal, and spiritual sins are judged according to shariah laws. Shariah courts were abolished in Tunisia in 1957, but Islamic fundamentalists are fighting to have them reinstated.

THE FIVE PILLARS OF ISLAM

The five pillars are: *shahadah*—professing faith ("There is no god but God, and Mohammed is his prophet"), *salat*—praying five times daily, *zakat*—giving alms (fixed at one-fortieth of personal income but voluntary today), *sawm*—fasting, and *hajj*—making the pilgrimage to Mecca.

Muslims wash in a prescribed way with water or sand before praying at dawn, midday, mid-afternoon, sunset, and nightfall. Facing in the direction of Mecca, the worshiper adopts three positions—standing, bowing, prostrating—symbolizing superiority of reason over instinct, as a servant before a master, and in submission before the will of God. Whenever possible, men gather to pray in a mosque under an *imam* (prayer leader); on Friday they are obliged to do so at noon. Prayer in a mosque is followed by a *khutba* (sermon). Women who attend public worship are segregated from the men. Most women prefer praying in the privacy of their homes.

Fasting throughout Ramadan, the ninth month of the Islamic calendar, is compulsory except for the sick, very young children, nursing mothers, pregnant women, the old, and travelers. Fasting means abstinence from eating, drinking, smoking, and sex from dawn to sunset.

Every Muslim should make the pilgrimage to Mecca at least once. During the *hajj*, Muslims dress in white seamless garments and abstain from shaving, cutting hair or nails, and sex. Rites performed during the *hajj* include kissing the sacred black stone, going around the Ka'abah, running seven times between the hills of Safa and Marwa, and standing in prayer at the Plain of Arafat.

ISLAMIC SECTS

In deciding on Mohammed's successor, or caliph (from *khalifah*, Arabic for "successor"), two Islamic factions arose that remain today: Sunni and Shi'a. The Sunnis believed caliphs should be elected and supported the first caliph, Abu Bakar, the Prophet's father-in-law. The Shi'as believed only the Prophet's direct descendants should rule. They supported Ali, the fourth caliph, the Prophet's cousin and son-in-law. Sunnis, the largest sect worldwide, follow the teaching in the Hadith.

Radical sects have also arisen over the centuries, among them Fatimids (a Shi'a group claiming descent from Fatima, the Prophet's daughter), Kharijites (a liberal sect, popular among poor Berbers, promoting the idea that any Muslim could be caliph), and the Sufis.

SUNNI ISLAM The Sunnis recognize four schools of Islamic law. The *Malikite* school is popular in North and Sub-Saharan Africa; the *Hanifite* school in Turkey, India, and China; the *Ibadi* school in Saudi Arabia;

A mosque in the desert. Five times daily, the *muadhdin* recites the call to prayer to the community over loudspeakers. Out of earshot, Muslims determine prayer time by the sun. The call states: "God is Great. I testify that there is no god but God. I testify that Mohammed is his prophet. Come to prayer. Come to security. God is great." In the morning the *muadhdin* adds, "Prayer is better than sleep."

A shrine for a local saint and a Berber pit home in an otherwise deserted landscape. As many as 100 whitewashed Sufi shrines exist in Nefta. An important Sufi master in Tunisia, Sidi Belhassen ech-Chadli, taught in a cave on Al Jellaz hill in Tunis in the 13th century. Two shrines, prohibited to non-Muslims, are Zaouia al Qadriya and the Koubba of Sidi Bou Ali. "Sidi" is an African Muslim title of respect for holy men. The towns of Sidi Bou Saïd, Sidi Merchrig, and Sidi Daoud are named after saints.

and the *Shafiite* school in Egypt, India, and Southeast Asia. These schools differ in the details of practice of Islam but do not question its dogmas. They came into existence in the second century of the Islamic era, when Muslim thinkers met to lay down shariah laws. Most Tunisian Muslims are of the Malikite school.

SUFISM This mystical sect originated in Persia in the 9th century A.D. *Suf* is Arabic for "wool," and the first Sufi believers wore woollen robes. Sufis are not satisfied to simply follow Islamic law. To bring them closer to God, they perform rituals including recitation, music, and dance. Many are ascetics who renounce materialism, believing that this brings a higher state of virtue. Their religious centers, or *zaouia*, are found mainly in the region of Nefta, north of Chott el Djerid. Sufis believe their masters possess *baraka* (blessedness or spiritual powers) and are marabouts (saints). Shrines are built above their graves, and their powers are believed to transfer to those who visit them.

KHARIJITES The Kharijite movement arose in Morocco to oppose Arab leadership of Islam, in particular the selection of the caliph based on race, station, or descent from the Prophet. The Kharijites proposed that any Muslim could be the religious leader. This idea appealed to the Berbers in Ifriqyya who resented the elite Arabs. Berber Kharijites invaded Kairouan during the rule of the Umayyads. They set up tribal kingdoms and fought the Abbasids (who followed the Umayyads).

The Kharijites continued to exist in great numbers until the 10th century when the Fatimids, another Islamic group, took control of Ifriqyya and began to persecute them. The Kharijites took refuge on Djerba Island where they live to this day. They are known for their austerity, and their 300-odd mosques on the island are simply designed.

FOLK BELIEFS AND SUPERSTITIONS

Folk beliefs have merged with Islam from the very early days of the religion. Many Muslims in Tunisia, for example, believe in the existence of spiritual powers (*baraka*) in some individuals, and that these are transferrable to others. They believe Mohammed had the most powerful *baraka*, and others who possess it are saints (marabouts). Proof of the possession of *baraka* is the performance of miracles, amazing spiritual insight, or bloodline connection to an earlier possessor of it.

In the past, marabouts were influential throughout the countryside as mediators in family and tribal disputes. Today, they have a role only in remote areas of central and southern Tunisia. These holy men built centers, where they taught, slept, and were buried. They had

The evil eye is widely feared and is warded off by simply holding out the fingers of the right hand. Many women wear the hand of Fatima (below) for protection.

followers or brotherhoods through which Islam spread rapidly in Tunisia. Sufism very likely developed out of some of these ideas.

In remote parts of Tunisia, superstitions stemming from ancient practices have blended with the practice of Islam. The idea of evil spirits called djinns, which often take the form of animals, is common. To protect themselves from djinns, some people wear amulets inscribed with Koranic verses; others toss bits of meat into dark corners to placate them. Certain stones are believed to possess magical properties; the bloodstone, for example, against a toothache. With the spread of education, superstitions are losing out to orthodox Islam in Tunisia.

JUDAISM

The history of the Jews is told in the Old Testament. The Jews believe that they are the "children of Abraham" (one of the founders of Judaism) and God's chosen people. Jewish sacred texts include the Torah (the first five books of the Bible attributed to the prophet Moses and written on parchment scrolls) and the Talmud (law and tradition).

The Ghriba Synagogue dates only to 1920 but the site goes back to 600 B.C., when according to legend a stone fell from heaven to dictate the location of the synagogue.

Jews have lived in Tunisia since ancient times. A small Jewish community of about 1,000 remain on Djerba Island, mainly as merchants or skilled craftspeople. The most famous synagogue in Tunisia is the Ghriba ("Marvelous") Synagogue on Djerba Island, one of the holiest Jewish places in North Africa; it is visited by Jewish pilgrims from around the world. A sacred cavern inside the synagogue contains one of the oldest Torahs in the world.

CHRISTIANITY

Christianity was the dominant religion in Tunisia in the Roman and Byzantine periods of rule. In A.D. 170 a Latin church was built in Carthage, and the holy scriptures were taught in Latin. Until the arrival of the Arabs, Tunisia was a major cultural and religious center for the Christian West. In A.D. 256, about 80 bishops met at a council in Carthage.

Christianity was never a religion of the poor masses in Tunisia, being popular mainly among the educated and rich—the ruling class or property owners. Then a group called the Donatists began espousing the cause of the poor. The Donatists came into existence in Tunisia when a conflict arose over the ordination of a bishop, Caecilian, in Carthage in A.D. 312. (The Donatists supported Caecilian's rival Donatus.) They were a dominant Christian group in the 4th century, known particularly for their martyrdom during the period of their persecution from A.D. 317 to 321. The group faded away gradually after a conference in Carthage in A.D. 411 denied the Donatists civil and ecclesiastical rights.

Cathedral of St. Vincent de Paul in Tunis. Many of the churches in Tunisia were established by the French and Italian communities in the north.

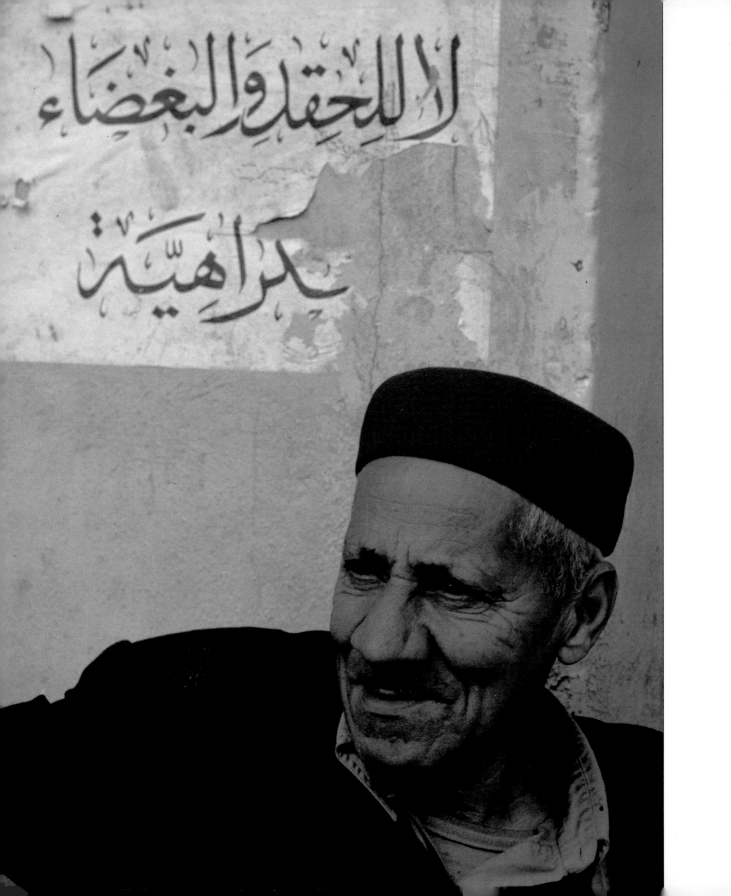

LANGUAGE

ARABIC, TUNISIA'S OFFICIAL LANGUAGE, is universally understood in the Maghrib. Tunisia's second language is French, which is widely used in government and business and is important socially. Spoken by half the population, French is a mark of sophistication and education. But while the bilingual, educated elite correspond in French, advertisements directed at the average Tunisian are in Arabic.

The Berber language is spoken by less than one percent of the population.

ARABIC

Four varieties of Arabic are used in Tunisia: classical, modern literary (or modern standard), colloquial (dialect), and intermediary (or "educated").

Classical Arabic is the language of the Koran and the ideal Muslims strive to achieve. As the vehicle of historical, literary, and religious heritage, it is used mainly for religious purposes.

Modern literary Arabic is a simplification of classical Arabic. In Tunisia it is the official language of the media, government documents, literature, and education. For most Tunisian adults, however, it is a language that can only be understood after formal study. The government has been promoting modern literary Arabic through lessons over television and radio, but without success.

Most Tunisians prefer intermediary Arabic. It is a mixture of colloquial and modern literary Arabic and is increasingly being used by the media, government, and intellectuals to communicate with the general population.

Opposite and below: **Tunisian Arabic is a combination of different forms and dialects. The Arabic of posters is likely to be "modern literary" while books such as the one above may use classical Arabic.**

Variations of Arabic dialect occur in Tunisia, but they are generally understood by all. Franco-Arabic, a weave of Arabic with specialized French terms and turns of speech, is an urban dialect spoken by students, government officials, and professionals. The urban and coastal dialects are closer to classical Arabic and similar to other dialects found in North African cities. In the interior, the Arabic dialect is heavily peppered with Berber words and has low prestige.

THE POLITICS OF LANGUAGE

The language issue has been given great attention in the Maghrib. Newly independent countries were determined to erase colonial influence by replacing the dominant European language with Arabic. Arabization, or the spread of Arab culture through language, has been more passionately promoted in other Maghrib countries than in Tunisia, where the policy has been a gradual spread of Arabic, while retaining the popular use of French. In the early years of self-government, the French-educated President Bourguiba promoted French to the extent that it created resentment. He then moderated his policies. Arabization has not been smooth in Tunisia. Modern literary Arabic was first chosen as the language of government and media, but most Tunisians did not understand it as it was spoken by a minority. The pragmatic government conceded that the friendlier intermediary Arabic was more useful. To be employed in the government, proficiency in modern literary Arabic is required, although French is used in internal communications. In medicine, technology, and science, French is essential.

THE LANGUAGE OF EDUCATION

In primary schools Arabic is the language of instruction; French is introduced as a second language in the third year. Secondary school students have a bilingual option; arts and social science subjects are taught in Arabic, while the sciences are taught in French. At the University of Tunis, French is the medium of instruction except for theology, law, and Arabic literature and language.

THE MEDIA

The government-owned Tunisian radio and television broadcasting station broadcasts in Arabic, French, and Italian over a national station, an international station, and five regional stations. Of the five television channels, the most popular is the French channel Antenne 2. Relay stations bring in Italian television programs. Radio Monte Carlo is the most popular station for music. For news, BBC World Service has a wide audience in Tunisia.

Media censorship is strict in Tunisia. Criticism of government officials or state institutions can bring seizure or suspension of the publication. Daily publications include the Arabic *As-Sabah* and *Al'Amal* and the French *L'Action*, *Le Temp*, and *La Presse*. Weekly newspapers and magazines include *Tunisia News*, *La Maghreb*, and *Jeune Afrique*.

Above: **French and Arabic signs outside this café in Tunis ensure that all potential Tunisian customers are well informed.**

Opposite: **Tunisians playing a board game on a sidewalk in Tunis are likely to speak a patois called "Frarabic," or Franco-Arabic. It is more often heard in Tunisia than pure Arabic or pure French.**

ARTS

TUNISIA'S ART TREASURES are the heritage of successive rulers of the country. Ancient crafts such as carpet weaving and pottery are important activities in Tunisia today, while a relatively new film industry is beginning to make its mark in the world of cinema.

ARCHITECTURE

PHOENICIAN Excavations at Cape Bon of Carthaginian houses on Byrsa Hill and a 5th century B.C. walled town in Kerkouane reveal that the Phoenicians may have based their models on Greek buildings. Tiled floors had inset pieces of marble, and walls were covered in stucco and Egyptian Pharaonic art. Punic temples also seem to be copied from the Greeks and Egyptians. The 3rd century Dougga Punic mausoleum, a pointed tower monument, is still intact.

ROMAN The hallmarks of Roman architecture can be seen in the Carthage aqueduct, El Djem amphitheater, theaters at Médenine, Chemtou, and Bulla Regia, and triumphal arches throughout Tunisia. The Romans developed cement and concrete and discovered how to build the arch and vault so that pillars were not needed to support the roof of a building. Only in the design of temples did they use the indigenous tradition of worshiping in an outdoor enclosure, as at the sanctuary of Saturn at Dougga. Some temples built by the Romans were dedicated to Moorish gods, but more often they were for Roman gods that were modifications of Phoenician gods. The god Baal Hammon, for example, became Saturn, who had a strong cult following in the countryside until the 5th century.

Opposite: **The crescent and star are Islamic symbols often repeated on the domes and doors of mosques. Decorations are focused on doors, floors, pillars, and lamps.**

Below: **Ulysses tied to a mast, a detail of a 3rd century A.D. mosaic from Dougga, found in the Bardo Museum.**

At Hergla, a loudspeaker on the minaret broadcasts the daily call to prayer. Windows are small, for unlike Western models, which emphasize the view outdoors, Islamic architecture focuses on privacy.

BYZANTIUM CHRISTIAN Byzantine architecture, seen in the churches, or basilicas, was inspired by the design of Roman public buildings. Church ruins at many sites (a famous one is Sbeïtla) come with naves, mosaic art, tombstones, altars, pillars, and baptisteries. The many fortresses built around forums, temples, and baths have helped preserve Roman sites. The most impressive ones can be seen at Haïdra, Ksar Lemsa, Mustim, Bordj Brahim, and Aïn Tounga.

ISLAMIC ARCHITECTURE The grandeur of Islamic architecture in Tunisia is seen in the mosques, shrines, public buildings, and homes of the wealthy, which are embellished with domes, minarets, and arches. The oldest Islamic buildings are ribats, or fortified monasteries.

The basic design of a mosque is a simple open courtyard, enclosed by a high windowless wall, that contains a fountain or wash area for the ritual cleansing before prayer. At the end of the courtyard is a roofed and carpeted prayer hall. Inside there is a mihrab, a niche indicating the direction of Mecca. In large mosques, there is also a minbar or pulpit where the prayer leader (imam) conducts special prayers on Friday. A minaret towers over the building. The basic plan has been modified over the centuries to include lodgings for visitors or students and classrooms for Koranic schools.

The first Tunisian mosques followed Byzantine church models, including their domes, arches, and high bell towers, which the Muslims used as minarets. The great mosques of Kairouan and Tunis are examples of Byzantine influence. There, the prayer halls are supported by rows of horseshoe-shaped arches resting on pillars salvaged from Roman buildings, and the buildings are topped by huge domes.

Later, there was a movement away from using highly decorated columns and capitals and toward clean pillars and arches. The new design focused on proportion, simplicity of form, elegant stonework, and calligraphic friezes. The great mosques of Sousse, Sfax, and Mahdia are examples of classical simplicity.

The Fadloum fortified mosque on Djerba Island. The early mosques built by armies fighting the holy war included features to help them repel attack—thick, windowless walls, powerful buttresses, battlements, and huge, solid doors.

In the 11th century, Moorish architecture was introduced under the Almohad and Hafsid caliphs. Most of the architecture of this period has been destroyed, but the Kasbah Mosque in Tunis is an excellent example of Moorish architecture. Under the 17th century beys, the Ottoman Turkish styles were imported: octagonal minarets, marble inlay, Andalusian tiles, Moorish carved plaster, and painted woodwork. In the flurry of decoration, proportion and simplicity were lost. The Husseinids favored external windows and decoration. The Tourbet el Bey, Mosque des Teinturiers, and the Sahib et Tabaa Mosque are a few examples.

TOWNS AND FORTIFIED BUILDINGS With the arrival of the Arabs in the 7th century, architectural design was influenced by the need for defensive features. A holy war was being fought. Early towns and villages were built with high surrounding walls with towers and thick gates, or *bab*.

Among the forts and citadels scattered throughout Tunisia is the Kef Kasbar on top of a hill. Monasteries (*ribat*), resting places for travelers (*fondouk*), and even buildings to store food were built defensively, some of them (the *ghorfa*, for example) by Berbers as defense against the Arabs.

Wealthy Tunisians have a room off the living room where male visitors are received without disturbing life in the courtyard. Walls are usually tiled.

HOMES AND PUBLIC BUILDINGS The plan of the North African house has been the same for many centuries. Rooms for eating, cooking, and sleeping are built around a courtyard used by the women of the house. The courtyard often has a well or cistern for water and is a private space screened from public view by a hall, zigzag passage, or screen. In the old days the courtyard had an arcade, while the rooms had plaster walls tiled in the lower half and painted wooden ceilings. Today, whitewashed concrete is the pragmatic choice.

MOSAICS

Bardo Museum has a rich collection of Roman mosaics dating from the 2nd to the 6th centuries A.D. The earliest known mosaic, discovered in Carthage, dates to the 5th or 4th century B.C. The Phoenicians first used this art form, and the Romans popularized it.

Roman mosaics of the early 1st century B.C. were simple and flat. Later they became more sophisticated and included geometric patterns. Some early African mosaics included polychrome panels in the borders, imported ready-made from Italy. Italian craftsmen brought over during this period to train people eventually set up their own workshops. Those at El Djem and Sousse were so successful that their mosaics decorated public buildings. Each workshop was known for its distinctive style.

The themes of mosaic art include the seasons, banquets, hunting, mythology, and gladiators. In Bulla Regia there is a mosaic of Venus borne by Tritons in a cockleshell flanked by two dolphins.

In this 3rd century mosaic from Sousse found in Bardo Museum, Virgil writes "The Aeneid." He is attended by Melpomene and Clio, who are muses, or Greek goddesses of the arts.

By the 2nd century A.D. mosaics were being produced in richer colors and with more complex compositions. In El Djem, mosaics decorated the Trajan Baths of A.D. 115–120 with a composition of Dionysus with satyrs, nymphs, and centaurs; the Thiasos Baths have a large marine scene. From the mid-3rd century A.D. production declined and form became more impressionistic and less detailed.

The golden age of mosaics was in the 4th and 5th centuries when an abstract style evolved with vivid stripes replacing subtle gradations of color. In the Christian era of the late 4th century mosaics were used to decorate churches. These often large and floral compositions were mainly geometric and included popular images such as scrolling vines and the Christian symbols of fishes and the Greek letters alpha and omega. Tomb mosaics, a form unique to Africa, also date to the Christian era. Often they had inscriptions, were nonfigurative (one example, in Kélibia, has ornamental borders and an epitaph in a crown flanked by a pair of palm trees), and sometimes had half or full-length portraits of the deceased, like those in Sfax and Tabarka.

CERAMICS

Tunisian pottery consists of figurines, jugs, and wall tiles. The Andalusian (Spanish Muslim) style most common today includes yellow, blue, and green patterns separated by bands of thick black lines, as well as by geometric designs. One of the most popular kinds is a shiny tile with metallic glints.

MODERN ART

The center of art is Tunis, where there are commercial galleries, state exhibition halls, an art school, and the Museum of Modern Art, which holds summer exhibitions.

Figurative painting in the 19th century focused on scenes from legends and formal court portraits of the ruling beys by Western artists. The first two native court painters were Ahmed Ben Osman and Hedi Khayouchi. In 1894 an art gallery was opened, but it showed mostly the work of European artists.

By 1912 a few Tunisian painters gained popularity, and eight years later a school was opened in Tunis to nurture local talent. A popular style imitated the ancient styles of Persian miniatures and glass painting that depicted scenes of daily life. The influence of expressionism and Fauvism (a French school favoring vivid colors in juxtaposition) modified Tunisian painting, resulting in the use of simple forms and a purity of color. Yahia Turki and Abdelaziz ben Rais were part of this new movement and are considered the fathers of modern Tunisian painting.

On Djerba Island, a potter turns the wheel in his shop. Nabeul, Moknine, and Djerba are famous for their potteries.

The independence struggle of the 1940s and 1950s influenced artists to create national styles. Hatem el Mekki experimented with various styles before using calligraphy. He created a fresh image for Tunisia by designing stamps, currency, and posters. Ammar Farhat painted detailed scenes of street life with symbols and metaphors from folk stories. The next generation of artists focused on more identifiable themes such as family loyalty, folk culture, and traditional lifestyles. Gouider Triki departed from such themes and created turbulent, colorful paintings full of strange figures: women with butterfly wings, men with bull or cockerel heads, and fish snakes whirling in wild dances. In 1994 he exhibited his works at the Institut du Monde Arabe in Paris.

CRAFTS

CARPETS, KILIMS, AND MERGOUMS Carpets are made of separate hand-knotted strands, while kilims and mergoums are woven as a single layer. Carpet-making is in the hands of a government-controlled agency that standardizes patterns and tags a carpet by the number of knots per square meter. Many Tunisian carpets have a white or light background with blue and red patterns similar to Berber and Persian designs. The carpets are often handwoven by children with small, delicate fingers. Large carpets take several years to make and can last several lifetimes.

Kilims have geometric patterns with lines broken by diamonds, lozenges, and zigzags. In mergoums, designs are emphasized by overstitching and embellishing with tassels and sequins. Themes include human and animal figures, Islamic legends, designs from Roman mosaics, and desert landscapes.

METALWORK, LEATHERCRAFT, AND WOODWORK Engraved brass and copper vases, ashtrays, plates, intricate wrought-iron window grilles, and blue and white birdcages are popular in Tunisia.

Like the other crafts, leather goods including sturdy and fashionable belts, saddles, and handbags can be found all over Tunisia, especially in the souks. Olive wood carved into bowls, spoons, chessboards, boxes, and sculptures are expertly made. Sfax, the olive oil capital, has the best selection.

Fish are a popular image in jewelry but also as tiles to decorate doors and walls.

CALLIGRAPHY AND IMAGERY

Text from the Koran is often the inspiration in Islamic art. Caliph Abdel Malik (A.D. 685–705) identified two schools of Arabic script: kufic and cursive. Kufic, an angular, solid, hieratic script, is suitable for carved and ornamental texts, while cursive is rounder and more flowing. Calligraphy is frequently used to decorate sacred books and the walls of religious buildings and is carved in stone and wood, and painted on ceramic tiles.

The development of calligraphy can be seen in early copies of the Koran. The oldest, from the 8th century, is written in a pronounced cursive style. Kufic, with interlacing stylized plant motifs, became the preferred religious script in the 9th century. The Bardo Museum has the 11th century blue Koran where verses are written in golden letters on blue parchment.

Images of fish and Fatima's hand are used in jewelry designs as they are believed to bring the bearer good luck. Fish symbolize fertility and the hand of Fatima is said to ward off evil. This stylized palm, with fingers outstretched, is worn by Muslim women.

CINEMA

In 1960 a film enthusiast and Arabic teacher, Tahar Cheriaa, set up the Tunisian Federation of Ciné Clubs. It is still the most important film directors' network in Africa. In 1964 the first cinema club opened in Tunisia and the Centre du Cinéma Tunisien that produced a few documentaries during its short life span.

After independence, Tunisia embarked on film production with its first coproduction of Jacques Baratier's film *Goha*, starring Claudia Cardinale and Omar Sharif. By 1966 the first Journée Cinématographiques de Carthage, the film festival in Carthage, was held, and just a year later an industrial film complex was created at Gammarth.

In the late 1960s, the Fédération Panafricaine des Cinéastes, a pan-African cinema federation of North and Black African directors, was formed. Being well established by then, Tunisian cinema developed a variety of genres ranging from comedy, political, and poetic to sociological and psychological. In 1994 Tunisian women entered the world of film directors when Moufida Tlatli's first feature film *The Silence of the Palace* won a prize at the Cannes Film Festival.

LITERATURE

Arabic is the main language of modern Tunisian literature, followed by French in novellas and plays. In the past, centers of Arabic literature included Kairouan, Mahdia, and Tunis. Subjects included praise for the rulers and theology. In the later years of Arab Tunisia, the focus shifted to Tunisia's African identity.

Recently, writers have been challenging the government and its policies through the novella. Laila ben Mami is a feminist voice in search of an end to women's oppression. The best known Tunisian writer is Albert Memmi, a Tunisian Jew living in Paris. He writes in French and his works are regularly translated into English.

Ibn Khaldun, born in Tunis in 1332, wrote the famous history of North Africa, *Al Muqaddim*, which explains the laws governing the rise and fall of Islamic dynasties. The work was translated into French in 1960.

LEISURE

TOURIST DOLLARS bring in a large portion of the country's income, so Tunisian leisure activities cater to the needs of tourists, who are mainly Europeans and Americans. Modern leisure activities include a wide range of water sports, tennis, golf, and hang gliding. Tunisians enjoy all of these, but they also love soccer and the centuries-old traditions of hunting and fishing. Country sports include horseriding along the beaches and trekking through the sandy mass of the Great Erb. Whatever the choice, there are activities for both the idle and the adrenaline-driven adventure-seeker.

Above: **Sailing dinghies at a holiday village in Hammamet. Water sports are very popular and there are many yacht berths and marinas for pleasure craft.**

Opposite: **Friends enjoy a board game in a street of Nabeul.**

WATER SPORTS

Blessed with roughly 700 miles (1,100 km) of coastland, gentle Mediterranean weather, and warm clear waters, Tunisia's abundant beaches in the north and along the eastern coast offer a plethora of activities on sand and surf. From rocky to sandy beaches, populous resorts to isolated beaches, Tunisians and tourists are spoiled for choice.

Tunisia enjoys a longer sailing season than the north Mediterranean countries and conditions for sailing are good all along the coast. Yachting marinas at Port El Kantaoui, Monastir, Sidi Bou Saïd, and Tabarka each have room for 200–400 vessels and the latest equipment, besides affiliation with resorts, hotels, restaurants, banks, shops, and other conveniences.

Snorkeling and scuba diving are popular activities, especially at Tabarka, an ancient coral trading center. There are diving centers for amateurs equipped with boats, professional instructors, diving monitors, and specialized gear in Monastir and the new seaside resorts in Tabarka, Port El Kantaoui, and Sousse.

Tunisians and tourists have a choice of swimming in the ocean or in countless hotel pools. Hotels often also rent equipment and offer instructors for water polo, water skiing, windsurfing, and parasailing.

The fishing and trading ports are frequented by regular fishers with advice to offer and stories to tell of their fishing adventures. Besides fish and shellfish, one can find octopuses off the Kerkenna Islands, sponges in the Gulf of Gabès, and coral on the Tabarka coast. Tuna fishing is especially good at Sidi Daoud on Cape Bon. River fishing is forbidden.

SOCCER

Tunisia has its own national, city, and village teams, and the country has competed in international tournaments such as the World Cup and the Mediterranean, Maghrib, Arab, and African leagues. Soccer is so infused in the cultural identity that even hotels have regular matches organized between staff and guests.

HUNTING

Children practice their soccer skills in a Tunis alley. Soccer is a passionate national pastime, and country-wide soccer matches kick off every Sunday.

Wild boar and game-bird hunting have been popular traditional sports in Tunisia for centuries. The wild boar season is from mid-October to the end of January, and hunting takes place in the dunes, hills, and mountains of the Kroumirie region.

The traditional hunting technique used is *battue* (French for "round up" or "beat") and it involves beating the bush to flush out wild boar. Firecrackers and dogs are used as well.

GOLF

Golf is an increasingly popular sport, and several major courses have recently been created in Tabarka, Hammamet, and Port El Kantaoui. The Port El Kantaoui golf course is of international standard, with 27 holes and three obstacle-filled courses.

SAND YACHTING

This activity is practiced on the dunes near Kébili and Douz. A land yacht is a three-wheeled boat with a sail, rudder, seat, and pedals.

HIKING

Tunisia has hiking trails in the mountainous north among the cork-oak covered Kroumirie mountains and on the gentle slopes of Zaghouan, Kasserine, Ain Durham, and El Kef. For those who prefer a different landscape, hiking trips across the desert south are also available. Walking four or five days across the Grand Eastern Erg is an experience for the fit and adventurous.

A brisk canter in Sousse. Horseback riding is a skill learned early in Tunisia.

HORSEBACK RIDING AND RACING

Horses are available for hire at beaches and hotels, and stables usually offer lessons and escorted rides. Some horse farms, such as the Baraket Stud Farm at Ghardimaou, near the Algerian border, offer treks for small groups. For those gambling on a windfall, there are horse races every Sunday at the Ksar Said and Monastir race courses.

THALASSOTHERAPY CENTERS

These centers are like ocean spas with sea water pools and therapists who use specialized fitness equipment. There are underwater massage baths, Jacuzzis, power and spray showers, bubbling gymnastic pools, massage booths, and mud and algae treatments. A whole range of treatments are offered, including beauty therapy, fitness and antistress treatment, alga-therapy, biomarine therapy and relaxation, postnatal therapy, and diet. The first one was built in Sousse at the Abou Nawas Boujaafar Hotel.

THERMAL SPRINGS

Traditionally healing waters draw the ailing and stressed. Three locations have been developed into healing centers: Hammam Bourguiba, between Tabarka and Ain Draham, has springs with waters prescribed for inflamed, infected, or allergic upper respiratory complaints; Korbous on Cape Bon has waters that cure chronic rheumatism, arthritis, and afflictions of the nervous system; and Djebel Oust in Zaghouan, with waters that treat rheumatism and other arthritic diseases.

SHOPPING TUNISIAN STYLE

Throughout Tunisia there are souks or bazaars. The more remote the area, the more important market day is as it provides an opportunity for a social gathering. In the countryside the souks are held in open fields and are known by the day on which the market is held, for example Souk el Femma (Friday's Souk) and Souk el Had (Sunday's market).

A souk, or bazaar, is filled with little shops or stalls, their goods spilling onto the sidewalk, selling anything from food and drink to rugs and perfume along a maze of narrow streets. Bargaining is a skill involving wit, humor, and acting ability. The locals know how to praise the goods without showing too keen an interest, and they begin by offering half the price quoted, then work their way up.

FESTIVALS

TUNISIA CELEBRATES secular holidays, Islamic feast days, and local festivals. The calendar of secular holidays was created after independence to draw people away from the purely religious identity of the country, and celebrations are state-organized and accompanied by speeches and parades. These holidays include the Anniversary of the 1952 Revolution on January 18, Independence Day on March 20, Martyr's Day (commemorating events of April 9, 1938), Republic Day on July 25, and Evacuation Day (commemorating the French evacuation from Bizerte on October 15).

ISLAMIC HOLIDAYS

Islamic feast days are very much a family celebration with some festivities spilling out onto the streets as people prepare for the holiday or socialize. The dates of Islamic holidays vary from year to year, the exact dates being calculated after the religious leaders have sighted the new moon. Three major Islamic holidays are Muharram (Islamic New Year), Eid al-Fitr, Eid al-Adha, and Mawlid an-Nabi.

Opposite: **Musicians and men on horseback on Djerba Island during a local festival. Such festivals celebrate the talents and traditions of towns and villages. Songs, poetry, and music are features of many traditional festivals.**

THE ISLAMIC CALENDAR

The Islamic era begins with Mohammed's flight from Mecca to Medina in 622 A.D. This journey is known as the Hegira, so dates are preceded by A.H. (Anno Hegirae, "year of the Hegira") rather that A.D. (the year of Christ's birth). The Islamic year is generally about 11 days shorter than the Gregorian year. The 12 months of the Islamic calendar are:

1. Muharram	4. Rabi at-tani	7. Rajab	10. Shawal
2. Safar	5. Jumadal-ula	8. Shaaban	11. Dhulkaeda
3. Rabi al-awwali	6. Jumadal-akira	9. Ramadan	12. Dhulhijja

EID AL-FITR Eid al-Fitr, the first day of the month of Shawal, celebrates the end of fasting and self-denial during the month of Ramadan. The day begins solemnly with prayer at the mosque, followed by a visit to the cemetery. Then festivities follow as families enjoy specially prepared food and wear new clothes. Gifts of money are given to children and newly married daughters. Gifts of food are given to the poor to break the fast and enjoy the celebration.

EID AL-ADHA This major festival is celebrated on the 10th of Dhulhijja and commemorates Abraham's willingness to sacrifice his son. The Koran stipulates that able heads of households purchase a sheep for sacrifice and share the meat of the animal with others—a third to the poor, a third to friends and neighbors, and a third to the family. This time of thanksgiving and charity is also an occasion for a family reunion.

The most sacred celebration takes place in Saudi Arabia in the small village of Mina, four miles (6.4 km) east of Mecca, where many thousands of Muslims take part in this sacrifice that marks the end of the hajj.

MAWLID AN-NABI Also known as Prophet Mohammed's birthday, it is celebrated on the 12th day of Rabi al-awwali, the third Muslim month. It was not observed until the ninth century of Islam when its exact date was determined. On this day of special prayer, men journey to the main mosque to hear stories of Mohammed's life told by the imam, or religious leader. Women usually gather at a friend's home for their own prayers. In Tunisia the festival is also celebrated with firecrackers.

A mosque in Tozeur is alight during Ramadan. Festivity pervades the air throughout the month-long fast, as Muslims visit the mosque in the evening for special prayers and shops remain open until late. Ramadan keeps Muslims in touch with the plight of the needy. It strengthens the spirit and increases endurance, while proving the strength of their faith.

TRADITIONAL FESTIVALS

Towns celebrate their own festivals. Some of these are Nabeul's Festival of Oranges, Testour's Festival of Malouf Music, Tabarka's Coral Festival, Sousse's theater and music festival, Dougga's festival of French classical theater, Kerkenna and Djerba islands' folklore festivals, Monastir's theater and poetry festival, and Tozeur's folklore festival. The Carthage International Cultural Festival is staged in a restored Roman theater where movies, dance, theater, and music are offered, mostly in French.

Haouaria, on the tip of Cape Bon, is a little village with a passion for falconry. At a falconry festival in June, when the village comes alive with concerts and dances, the falconers display their skills. Falconers train birds to hunt partridge and quail. The best hunters have mammoth appetites and speedy digestion. Trainers control the birds through affection and food.

The Tamerza Festival brings together the Berber communities. Held in April-May, this festival has exhibitions of ancient Berber arts and traditions, folk concerts, parades, theatrical performances, and horse displays.

Men on horseback carry rifles at a desert festival. At the desert festival in Douz (December to January), one can see camel fights, sand hockey, and greyhound racing.

FOOD

TUNISIAN CUISINE BLENDS North African spices with French and Italian influences. Common ingredients are olive oil, spices, rice, tomatoes, onions, seafood, and chicken or lamb. Meat is beyond the means of the average Tunisian family.

Tunisian dishes are served with a side dish of *harrissa* ("ha-RRI-sa"), a spicy paste made of ground dried chilis, spices, garlic, and olive oil; it is also a common ingredient of many Tunisian dishes.

The best food in Tunisia is found at the sides of streets where a great variety of freshly made food is sold. Open-air food stalls, cabins, and caravans sell Tunisian fast food—sandwiches filled with tuna, hardboiled egg, peppers, tomatoes, and onions, dressed with olive oil and some harrissa sauce. These fast food places are found near bus and railway stations and markets. The food is cheap and tasty, but customers cannot linger over a meal; they are expected to eat and leave.

Opposite: **A spice market in Douz. Markets in the country are often outdoors.**

Below: **Vegetables in couscous dishes change with the season—they can be broad beans, pumpkin, chickpeas, turnip, or carrot. Other ingredients may be chicken, fish, or osben (sausage filled with tripe and herbs).**

In the desert near Tamerza, a woman cooks while her family waits in the shade of their home.

A GLOSSARY OF TUNISIAN DISHES

A deep-fried savory pastry dish called *brik* usually has a runny egg inside. Other fillings include spicy potato, prawns, anchovies, spinach, and tuna. It is eaten by hand, often dipped in harrissa.

Chakchouka ("shahk-SHOO-ka") is a spicy vegetable stew of tomatoes, onions, and pimentos (grilled sweet red peppers) with an egg on top. *Chorba* ("SHOHR-ba") means soup. Chorba Tunisienne is a soup with tomatoes, onions, harrissa, and pasta. Fresh chorba de poisson (fish soup) is a favorite. Fish is usually served grilled with olive oil and lemon juice; it may also be fried, baked, or stuffed. Fresh seafood is often served with a grilled salad of sweet red peppers, tomatoes, onions, and garlic.

Couscous, the national dish, is served for lunch and dinner. It is made by partially baking semolina flour with water, then grinding it into a fine grain. This is followed by steaming and oiling to separate the grains. Spices added to couscous vary with the region, from cinnamon to dried, crushed rosebuds. *Couscous* is eaten with vegetables and meat ladled on top—perhaps *Kaftaji* ("kahf-TAH-ji"), spicy meatballs garnished with chopped liver, onions, peppers, and zucchini, or *Kamounis* ("kah-MOO-nis"), a meat stew flavored with cumin.

Maarcassin ("mahr-KAH-sin")—wild boar served with a dark sauce—is common during the winter hunting season. Eating pork and drinking wine may offend others in this predominantly Islamic country, so in restaurants a screen is put up to mask this activity from those who might object. *Mechoui* ("muh–SHWEE") is grilled meat, often lamb and sometimes liver and sausages. *Menchouia* ("muhn-SHWEE-uh"), or spicy grilled vegetables (onions, peppers, and tomatoes) dressed with olive oil), is garnished with tuna and hardboiled eggs. *Merguez* ("muhr-GWEH") are small mutton and harrissa sausages.

Ojja ("OH-sjah") are eggs scrambled with onions, peppers, tomatoes, and slices of spicy sausage. *Tajine* ("tah-JEEN"), a cake made of eggs and chopped meat, seasoned with parsley, cheese, or pimentos, is best eaten hot, but can be served as cold slices with sauce on top.

In Tunisia desserts are not necessarily eaten at the end of a meal. Sweets are usually savored over conversation, often with a refreshing glass of mint tea.

DESSERTS

Tunisian *baklava*, like the Greek version of the sweet, has layers of pastry filled with nuts and soaked in honey. Another common sweet is *Makrud* ("mahk-ROOD"), a semolina cake soaked in honey with dates in the center. *Bouza* ("BOO-za") is a dessert of hazelnut or sorghum cream with grilled sesame seeds. *Assida* ("ah-SEH-da") is a thick flour cream with grilled pine seeds, but pistachio, hazelnut, and pine kernels can be used as well.

Mint tea, made by pouring fresh hot water over a handful of mint leaves, is the national drink. It is sometimes served with pine kernels and always with lots of sugar and no milk.

DRINKS

Alcohol is prohibited to Muslims, but tourists may order alcoholic drinks in bars and restaurants. Tunisia produces its own wine, a tradition cultivated since the time of the Phoenicians. Tunisian wines come from vineyards in the north. Tunisian-made liqueurs include the fig-based Thibarine, a distilled fig wine called Boukha, and Laghami, or fermented date palm sap.

NONALCOHOLIC THIRST QUENCHERS Tunisian tap water is safe but many prefer bottled spring water. Tunisia bottles mineral water under the labels Safia, Ain Garci, Selma, Jetkiss, and Zulel.

Freshly squeezed fruit juices are the most popular drinks in Tunisia. Orange and lemon juice are especially popular in the summer. In Tunisian homes one can also find huge containers full of homemade carrot juice and the triple concoction of orange, lemon, and grapefruit.

TEA AND COFFEE Tea is so much a part of the Tunisian lifestyle that wherever two or three Tunisians gather there must be a beaten old pot brewing tea over a charcoal fire. Tea is served strong; sometimes people discard the teaspoon and choose instead to bite on chunks of sugar then strain the tea through the sugar in their mouth. Coffee is served Turkish style—cooked fresh in small pots and served strong and black with the grounds in the cup. While waiting for the grounds to settle Tunisians engage in conversation. Tunisian coffee is sometimes flavored with cardamom.

Market day in Nefta is a time to socialize as well as to shop.

HARRISSA

(Makes a quarter cup and keeps for up to three months.)

20 dried New Mexico or guajillo chilies
cayenne powder to taste
1/4 to 1/2 teaspoon freshly ground, dry-roasted caraway seeds
1 1/2 to 2 teaspoons freshly ground, dry-roasted coriander seeds
1 very small garlic clove, chopped
1/4 teaspoon salt, or to taste
3 tablespoons olive oil, and more to cover the paste

1. Wearing rubber gloves, rinse the chilies. Pull off the stems, seed, and soak the chilies in cold water until softened.

2. Drain well, pressing out excess water.

3. In a food processor, blend chilies with all other ingredients except oil.

4. Add olive oil and blend until smooth. Pack into a jar and cover with a layer of oil. Keep refrigerated.

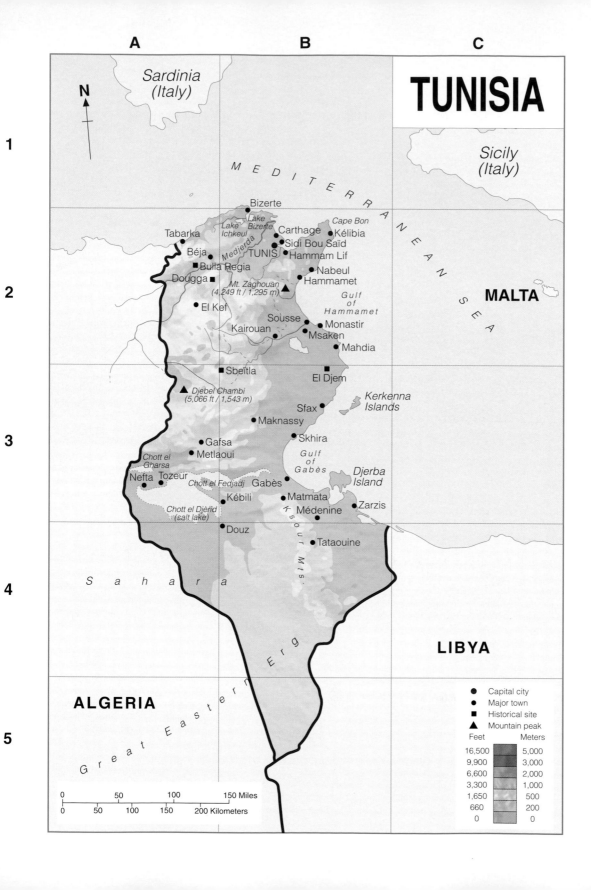

TUNISIA

Sardinia (Italy)

N

1

Sicily (Italy)

M E D I T E R R A N E A N   S E A

MALTA

Bizerte

Lake Ichkeul *Lake Bizerte* *Cape Bon*

Tabarka Carthage Kélibia

Béja Sidi Bou Saïd

Medjerda TUNIS Hammam Lif

■ Bulla Regia Nabeul

Doùgga ■ *Mt. Zaghouan (4,249 ft / 1,295 m)* ▲ Hammamet

2

● El Kef *Gulf of Hammamet*

Sousse

Kairouan ● Monastir

Msaken

■ Sbeïtla ● Mahdia

■ El Djem

▲ *Djebel Chambi (5,066 ft / 1,543 m)*

Sfax *Kerkenna Islands*

Maknassy

3 Skhira

Gafsa *Gulf of Gabès*

Metlaoui *Djerba Island*

Chott el Gharsa

Nefta Tozeur Gabès

Chott el Fedjadj

Kébili Matmata Zarzis

Médenine

Chott el Djèrid (salt lake)

Douz

Tataouine

4

S a h a r a

LIBYA

Great Eastern Erg

ALGERIA

5

● Capital city
● Major town
■ Historical site
▲ Mountain peak

Feet		Meters
16,500		5,000
9,900		3,000
6,600		2,000
3,300		1,000
1,650		500
660		200
0		0

0   50   100   150 Miles

0   50   100   150   200 Kilometers

QUICK NOTES

OFFICIAL NAME
Republic of Tunisia
Arabic: Al-Jumhuriyah at-Tunisiyah

CAPITAL
Tunis

MAJOR CITIES
Sfax, Sousse, Bizerte, Kairouan

LAND AREA
63,378 square miles (164,419 square km)

HIGHEST POINT
Djebel Chambi (5,066 ft/1,543 m)

MOUNTAIN RANGES
Northern Tell and Dorsale (High Tell)

MAIN RIVER
Medjerda (286 miles/460 km)

FLAG
A red crescent and a red five-pointed star within a white disk centered on a red background

ANTHEM
Al-Khaladi ("The Glorious")

MONEY
One Tunisian Dinar (D) = 1,000 millimes. Coins of 1, 2, 5, 10, 20, 50, and 100 millimes. Notes come in half, 1, 5, 10, and 20 dinars.
D1 = US$1.28

MAIN EXPORTS
Petroleum, phosphates, olive oil

MAIN IMPORT
Food

OFFICIAL LANGUAGE
Arabic and French
French is the language of business

POPULATION
8,882,000 people (1994 census)

RELIGION
Islam (98%), Christianity (1%),
Judaism (1%)

SECULAR PUBLIC HOLIDAYS
New Year's Day—January 1
Anniversary of the 1952 Revolution—
    January 18
Independence Day—March 20
Martyr's Day—April 9
Labor Day—May 1
Victory Day—June 1
Republic Day—July 25
Women's Day—August 13

ISLAMIC PUBLIC HOLIDAYS (VARIABLE)
Muharram (Islamic New Year)—
    first of the month of Muharram
Eid al-Fitr—first of Shawal
Eid al-Adha—10th of Dhulhijja
Mawlid an-Nabi (Prophet Mohammed's
    birthday)—12th of Rabi al-awwali

GLOSSARY

Arabization
The spread of Arab culture, mainly through the use of Arabic.

bab ("BEHB")
Gate.

baraka ("BAH-ra-kah")
Spiritual powers.

Berber
Indigenous people of North Africa.

bey ("BAY")
Ruler of Tunis, the title adopted by the monarch of Tunisia. The monarchy was made obsolete in 1957, after Tunisia became independent.

chehili ("shair-HI-li")
Hot southerly winds that bring sand blizzards.

Chott ("SHOT")
Salt lake. Sometimes spelt "shott" or "shatt."

Djebel ("shjehr-BUHL")
Hill or mountain.

Eid ("EED")
Festival. Two major Islamic festivals in Tunisia are Eid al-Fitr and Eid al-Adha.

ghorfa ("GHOR-fa")
Arabic for "room," a storage area for grain.

harrissa ("ha-RRI-sa")
Paste of chilies, garlic, spices, and olive oil used as a dip and also as an ingredient in Tunisian cooking.

Ifriqyya
Arabic name for the region of Tunisia, the area of which changed frequently in history.

Kharijites
Members of an Islamic movement that began in Morocco. In Tunisia, they are a small group living mainly on Djerba Island. The Kharijites opposed selecting a caliph on the basis of race, station, or descent from the Prophet Mohammed.

ksar ("SAHR")
Arabic for "fortress," a fortified granary.

Maghrib
North African Arab states including Morocco, Algeria, Tunisia, and sometimes Libya.

medina ("muh-DI-na")
Old section of cities, usually featuring narrow alleys lined with houses, shops, and mosques.

ribat ("ri-BAHT")
Fortress built by Muslim rulers.

sahel ("sair-HELL")
Shore or coast. The Sahel refers to the coastal region in eastern Tunisia.

sidi ("see-DI")
"Master," title of respect reserved for holy men.

souk ("SOOK")
Bazaar or open-air market.

zaouia ("zo-EE-ya")
Center of a religious brotherhood such as of the Sufi sect of Islam.

BIBLIOGRAPHY

Fox, M.R., *Enchantment of the World: Tunisia*. Chicago: Children's Press, 1988.

Klotchkoff, Jean-Claude and Melissa Thackway (translator). *Tunisia Today*. Paris: Les Editions du Jaguar, 1995.

Nelson, Harold D. (ed.). *Tunisia: A Country Study*, 3rd edition. Foreign Area Studies, The American University for the Area Handbook Series. Washington D.C: Department of the Army, 1988.

Tunisia: 40 Years After independence. Tunis: Carthage Multimedia, 1996.

Tunisia in Pictures. Minneapolis: Lerner Publications Company, 1992.

Zghal, Riadh, "Tunisia: They Do It Their Way," *Unesco Courier*, April 1994.

INDEX

INDEX

INDEX

PICTURE CREDITS